RECORDS MANAGEMENT

A Practical Approach

Third Edition

Susan Z. Diamond

ama·om

American Management Association

New York • Atlanta • Boston • Chicago • Kansas City • San Francisco • Washington, D.C.
Brussels • Mexico City • Tokyo • Toronto

Library of Congress Cataloging-in-Publication Data

Diamond, Susan Z.
    Records management : a practical approach / Susan Z.
Diamond—3rd ed.
        p.   cm.
    Includes bibliographical references and index.
    ISBN 0-8144-0295-X
    1. Records—Management.   I. Title.
    HF5736.D48   1995
    651.5—dc20   95-4604
                                                          CIP

Printing number

10   9   8   7   6   5   4   3   2   1

To
Allan

Contents

Preface

As I began preparing the third edition of this book, several thoughts came to mind. First, while the basic principles of records management are unchanged, implementing them has become more difficult. In this age of "reengineering" and "downsizing," everyone, including the records manager, is wearing multiple hats. Therefore, today's records managers have less time and fewer resources to accomplish their objectives. As a result, in this edition, I've tried to emphasize the most critical program components and simplify the overall processes whenever possible.

Second, in the four years since the second edition was published, the technology and resources available to the records manager have changed even more than they did in the seven years between the first and second editions. These changes offer enormous potential to the records manager, but also provide a real challenge. The records manager has to define his or her role as part of the office automation team. By working with users and the systems staff, the records manager can make major contributions to overall productivity.

The ideas in this book have been tested repeatedly through my consulting practice and communicated to thousands of participants in the records management seminars I conduct. I am grateful to all of the individuals I've worked with for the interchange of ideas, as well as for the continued enthusiasm and support for this book.

Thanks are due to Tony Vlamis, my editor at AMACOM and the motivating force behind this third edition. I am also grateful to the following companies for providing the photographs for this edition: Commercial Archives, Filenet Corporation, Spacesaver Corporation, and TAB Products Co.

Finally, this book is dedicated to Allan, my husband and partner for almost twenty-five years. His new role in managing the day to day operations of our business has allowed me to concentrate on my consulting, training, and writing activities. Without his support, this book's deadline and many others would not have been met.

1

What Is Records Management?

Records management—the words conjure up a variety of meanings: "a fancy name for filing," the storage of inactive records, the computerization of information, document imaging, records retention schedules. Actually, records management is all of the above and much more. And while the concept has been around for a number of years, many organizations—some quite large—still do not have a viable records management program. Others have allowed their programs to become dormant. Before considering how to establish or revitalize a program, we need to determine exactly what records management is and why every organization—large or small—needs it.

Defining Key Terms

Let's begin with some definitions. A "record" is any form of recorded information. The means of recording the information may be paper, microfilm, audiotapes, videotapes, photographs, slides, or any computer-readable medium such as computer tapes or disks, compact disks, or optical disks. In other words, practically any information created or communicated within the organization, except unrecorded conversations, forms a record.

Records typically have a four-stage life cycle. First, there is creation, when pen is put to paper, data is generated by a computer, or information is captured on film, tape, or any other medium. Next is the period of active use, which can range from a few days to several years. During this period, users frequently reference the record and need quick access to it. Consequently, the record is maintained in the office area. Most records have an active life of one to two years, although there are some obvious exceptions. For example, a personnel file is active as long as the employee is on staff.

The third period in the cycle is when the record is inactive and in storage. During this period, the record is kept either because of legal reasons or because of users' infrequent reference needs. Some records may have no inactive period, while others may remain in this stage for several years or even "permanently" (that is, for the life of the organization).

The final stage in the cycle is destruction, which occurs when the organization no longer needs the record and is no longer required by law to keep it. With confidential or proprietary records, special precautions must be taken to ensure that destruction is total and the records can in no way be recreated.

A common misconception is that records management involves only the latter two stages of a record's life. In reality, records management is concerned with controlling records from their creation, through both active and inactive periods to their destruction. When properly implemented, this total concept means preventing the creation of unnecessary records and unnecessary extra copies; ensuring the efficient, economical use of records in both the active and inactive periods; and destroying records as soon as they're not needed. Thus, records management promotes the efficient retrieval and use of information, while keeping records maintenance costs to a minimum.

Records Management Is . . .

With the comprehensive definition I've just outlined, records management becomes a broad-based discipline comprised of the following areas:

- *Records retention* to ensure that records are kept only as long as they are needed for operational, legal, fiscal, or historical purposes.
- *Storage of inactive records* in a way that ensures their speedy retrieval.

- *Protection of vital records,* those records essential to the organization's continued existence.
- *Creation and implementation of filing systems* to manage active paper records.
- *Utilization of document imaging technologies* such as micrographics and EDI (electronic document imaging). The responsibility for electronic imaging will, however, be shared with the systems department.
- *Forms management* through the proper design and use of forms—one way of controlling records from their creation.
- *Reports management* through the effective design and use of reports—another way to control records from their creation.

Although some organizations' records management programs do not encompass all of these areas, ideally they should all be grouped together to enhance their overall effectiveness. For example, forms management is most effective when it is part of records management. Not only are the overall goals of both programs quite similar, but poorly designed forms can create major problems in the filing, document imaging, and records storage areas.

Some definitions of records management are even broader, encompassing IS (information systems), mail and messenger service, the print shop, copiers, and so on. The argument is that the records manager should manage all aspects of organizational information and communications regardless of form. While one individual may manage all of these areas, they are not part of records management per se. The records manager does, of course, interact closely with these areas. However, saying they are part of records management is as illogical as saying that all employees should report to the human resources manager because he or she manages personnel.

Benefits of Records Management

Instituting a records management program results in both immediate and long-term benefits to the organization. These benefits include:

▪ *Faster retrieval of information.* Retrieval speed is improved both through the use of non-paper-based technology and better management of paper records systems.

▪ *Fewer lost or misplaced records.* Because the human element is always with us, even the best system in the world will occasionally have a misplaced record. But properly designed document management systems reduce misfiles substantially, and a misfiled record can cost as much as $150 in terms of time spent searching for the record. Keep in mind, too, that records can be "misplaced" on the computer through inaccurate indexing or data entry.

▪ *Compliance with legal retention requirements.* Organizations without a records management program run the risk of destroying records too soon and, consequently, of not being able to produce them when legally required. Or else they adopt the costly practice of keeping everything forever—a practice that can also backfire in a legal proceeding. The organization is then required to produce everything it has relating to the proceeding, not just what it is legally required to have. At the very least, producing all related records is time consuming and expensive. And depending on the nature of the records, doing so may jeopardize the organization's case through the admission of unfavorable evidence.

▪ *Space savings.* Implementing a records retention schedule and destroying unnecessary and duplicate records can conserve up to 40 percent of the space occupied by records. The effective use of document imaging systems and high density filing equipment provides further space savings.

▪ *Reducing expenditures for filing equipment and supplies.* Eliminating unnecessary records and using nonpaper media can cut costs dramatically in this area.

▪ *Controlling the creation of new records.* Both forms and reports management reduce the amount of records that are created internally while improving their effectiveness.

▪ *Protecting the organization's vital records.* Any organization is vulnerable to disaster. The accidental destruction of essential records can cost an organization millions of dollars or even prove fatal to its continued existence. A vital records program ensures that the organization has protected copies of essential records.

The list of benefits provided by a comprehensive records management program is a formidable one. Altogether, these benefits meet the dual goals of increased efficiency and reduced expense, and thus they more than justify the cost and effort required to establish a records management program.

2

Getting Support for the Records Management Program

In spite of the benefits records management provides, quite a few records managers find their biggest problem is not in implementing the program, but in convincing others of the need to implement it and support it on an ongoing basis. Two groups must be "sold" on the concept: (1) senior management and (2) the primary users of the program—middle and lower management and their staffs. Each group has different concerns, and you must modify your "sales pitch" accordingly.

Selling the Program to Senior Management

We'll start with senior management as their support is essential for obtaining the necessary resources. If senior management isn't interested in the program, you need to determine why before trying to sell the program. Usually one or more of the following factors is the root of the disinterest:

Ignorance of the records management concept. Most members of senior management are only vaguely aware of what records management involves. Consequently, one of the first steps is to "educate" them in this area by explaining what records management is and the benefits it provides.

Misunderstanding about the "M-word"—money. Senior management often feels records management is not "cost justified." They perceive the program as requiring substantial initial cash outlays with little or no return on the investment. While records management is not a "profit center," it does save money through greater productivity, more effective use of office space, and reduced expenditures for filing equipment and supplies. Once the savings are emphasized, top executives become much more receptive to records management.

Another good argument is to point out the value of the records themselves. One vice president of research and development pointed out that "these records are all we have to show for seventeen million dollars of research. We'd better spend some money to protect them and increase their usefulness."

Fear of "empire building." Today many businesses emphasize decentralization. In such organizations, it's easy to view records management as the "records police" or to assume that the records manager is trying to gain control at the expense of productivity. While there are a few records managers who misconstrue their role and are totally inflexible, most records managers are merely trying to provide good service while protecting valuable information from loss or destruction.

To defuse charges of "empire building," it helps to compare records management to the human resources and finance areas. No organization would give each department head a checkbook and say "pay your own bills." Nor would it let each manager run employment advertisements in the paper and hire people at any salary level he or she wanted to. In other words, some necessary controls have already been placed over two of an organization's most valuable resources, money and people. Records management is a similar control over the third key resource, information.

The records management function also provides in-house expertise in a technical area. It is not realistic to expect each department head to be an expert in records management, any more than you would expect them to be an expert in human resources or finance.

Ignorance of the organization's legal vulnerability if it doesn't have a program. As legal protection, records management is similar to an insurance policy. You hope you never have to use it, but if you do, you're really glad you have it. When companies are involved in litigation, fast, complete retrieval of relevant records is essential. Also, a consistent records management program helps protect the company from charges of destroying or misplacing records to conceal information. In fact, the records manager may even be required to testify about the company's record retention policies and procedures. Because of these factors, many organizations belatedly establish records management after litigation occurs. Of course, a little forethought in this area would have saved them considerable effort and expense in document production.

Unawareness of problems that exist. In other words, "we've always managed just fine without a records management program." Senior management rarely has a problem obtaining records. They usually have the best secretaries and administrative support in the organization. When they need a record, they get it. Heaven and earth may have moved to provide that record, but the executive is blissfully unaware of that fact.

Also symptoms of a records management problem such as a shortage of office space, rising copier costs, and increased filing equipment expenditures are rarely linked together. Instead, they are treated separately through such remedies as adding more computers, open plan offices, new types of filing equipment, and copier controls. While these solutions may be advisable, the first step should be to deal with the underlying problem—the lack of records management.

Shaping a Strategy

After you've determined why your management either has not established a program or allowed an existing program to become inactive or ineffective, you can develop an appropriate strategy to correct the situation.

As you develop your strategy, keep in mind the needs and concerns of the people you must convince. For example, if management is concerned with being "state of the art," emphasize the technological aspects of the program and let them know what other companies in their industry have done.

On the other hand, if management is conservative in its approaches or resistant to change, emphasizing the legal problems the company can encounter without records management is helpful. With this type of management, it's also helpful to let them know what other companies have done. Some ways of doing this are arranging a visit to a company with a comprehensive, well-run records management program, providing appropriate articles on the subject, and attending a local meeting of ARMA International (Association of Records Managers and Administrators, International). Providing reinforcement through examples of what other organizations are doing is important because it defuses any management suspicions of "empire building," as well as substantiates your recommendations.

Another powerful selling point is ISO 9000 certification. Many organizations are working to obtain this international quality certification, which aids in marketing the firm's products or services. While the ISO 9000 series standards do not specify requirements for records management, they do require that the organization have a records management program in place and that retention periods be specified for records. In a recent seminar I taught, almost 50 percent of the participants were there because their organizations were trying for ISO 9000 certification.

For many companies, cost justification is a prime concern. In this case, it helps to document expenditures for filing equipment over the past five years and the cost of the office space now occupied by that filing equipment. Then point out that implementing a records management program will make approximately 40 percent of the space available for other uses and may eliminate purchasing filing equipment for several years.

Also, any significant capital expenditure should be cost justified. Cost-benefit analyses will be discussed throughout this book in relation to each aspect of the program. Showing senior management your understanding of economic realities is extremely important in getting financial support for the program.

Virtually all aspects of records management save money, except for vital records protection. Since this area involves storing duplicates of vital records off site, it does cost money. However, I present vital records protection as a form of insurance that is just as important as insuring the business's property and equipment.

One last psychological point—don't criticize the company's previous records management practices, or lack thereof. The people you are trying to convince sanctioned those practices. Instead, take the approach that the existing system undoubtedly met the organization's needs initially but is no longer adequate in view of the changing legal climate, increased cost of office space, and so on.

Gathering Additional Data

If you're still encountering resistance to establishing a program, surveying current records management practices within the organization should provide you with the data that you need to get support. The survey is not a comprehensive study of the organization's records; that comes later when you're preparing the retention schedule. Instead, this survey identifies major records problems within the organization, as well as providing some statistical data for the program.

While the data can be gathered through interviews, unless you're with a very small organization, interviewing will be too time consuming. Surveying the departments through a questionnaire will usually be more practical. Exhibit 2-1 is a sample of such a questionnaire. One caution here: Keep the questionnaire short and simple. You simply want enough data to gain support for the program. While conducting "in-depth" studies is very popular today, often the time spent "studying" the situation could be better applied to solving the problem.

After you've gathered the responses, you should be able to come up with some effective, attention-getting statistics. For example, one records manager I know pointed out to the board of directors that there were seven file drawers of records for every office employee. She went on to explain that reducing the records volume to three and a half drawers per employee would free up enough floor space for eleven additional clerical workstations. Since the company is growing rapidly and short of space, she got management's attention very quickly.

You'll also be able to identify which departments generate the most records, which are experiencing the most growth in records volume, and which are having problems or are poorly organized. In most organizations, approximately one-half of the records are in the finance and accounting area. Depending on the organiza-

Exhibit 2-1. Departmental Records Management Survey (no program in place)

Dept. Name	Dept. No.
Survey Completed By	Date

1. What volume of paper records are now maintained in your department? Indicate the number on the appropriate line(s).

    _____ file drawers   _____ shelves

    _____ boxes (please give box size: _____)

    _____ other: _____

2. Has the volume of records increased in the past year?

    ☐ Yes ☐ No   If yes, by what amount? _____

3. If you know, state approximately how much money your department has spent on filing equipment and supplies in each of the past three years.

    1995: _____ 1994: _____ 1993: _____

4. On an average, how many years of records does your department maintain in the office area?

    ☐ 1 to 2   ☐ 3 to 4   ☐ 5 to 7   ☐ 8 or more yrs.

5. Who is responsible for filing records in the department?

    ☐ Administrative assistants and/or secretaries

    ☐ Everyone does his or her own filing.

    ☐ Other: _____

6. If you have any written filing procedures, files indexes, etc., please attach a copy.

7. Is the department experiencing any problems with its records?

    ☐ Yes ☐ No

    If yes, please indicate the type of problem:

    ☐ Lost or missing files   ☐ Lack of space for records

    ☐ Filing backlogs   ☐ Other: _____

    Thank you for completing the survey!

tion, other high volume areas are research, customer records, legal, human resources, and engineering. The high volume, high growth areas are usually your best candidates for converting records to another medium such as microfilm or optical disk, as well as offering the greatest potential for space savings through disposition of unnecessary and duplicate records.

Areas that are poorly organized and are experiencing problems with their record keeping should be a high priority for attention. Of course, the politics of the situation will affect this as well. A department that realizes it has problems and wants help will be much easier to work with than one that feels it has no problems. And since you want to build credibility for the program through successes, start with the people who want help.

If, instead of starting from scratch, you've inherited an existing program, you may want to begin by surveying departments to find out what parts of the program are working for them. Obviously, the nature of this survey will depend on the kind of program in place, but Exhibit 2-2 is a typical sample.

When you review this data, you're trying to determine who is aware of the program and complying with it. Be careful though. If people feel the questionnaire's purpose is to "trap" them, they may not reply honestly. Make sure everyone understands that the purpose of the survey is to improve the records management program, not to get users in trouble. Then, once you've reviewed the surveys and identified the problem areas, you can turn your attention toward correcting them.

Developing an Action Plan

As any records manager with a good program can tell you, establishing a full-scale program usually takes years. However, before you panic or consider the task hopeless, you should also realize that within one year significant improvements can be made and a firm foundation laid for the overall program. And if you can't show results in that time period, management is likely to consider the program a failure.

Your first step is identifying what needs to be done and establishing priorities. If the organization does not have a records retention schedule or if the schedule has not been revised within the

Exhibit 2-2. Departmental Records Management Survey (program already in place)

Dept. Name	Dept. No.
Survey Completed By	Date

1. Does your department have a copy of the corporate records manual?
   ☐ Yes ☐ No

2. Are the records maintained in the office purged regularly in accordance with the retention schedule?
   ☐ Yes ☐ No
   Who does it? _____(job title)

3. Are electronic (i.e., computer) files also purged regularly?
   ☐ Yes ☐ No

4. Does your department send inactive records to the corporate records center?
   ☐ Yes ☐ No If yes, how often?
   ☐ Monthly ☐ Quarterly ☐ Annually ☐ Other:_____

5. How frequently does your department retrieve records from the corporate records center?
   ☐ Weekly ☐ Monthly ☐ Quarterly ☐ Annually ☐ Never

6. If you retrieve records, how long does it normally take to receive a record?
   ☐ 4 hrs. or less   ☐ 4 to 8 hrs.   ☐ longer than 1 day

7. Have you ever not received a record you requested?
   ☐ Yes ☐ No   If yes, how often in the past year?
   ☐ Once   ☐ Twice   ☐ 3 or more times
   What reason was given? _____

8. Do you have any comments or suggestions for improving the records management program?
   _____
   _____
   _____
   _____
   _____

   Thank you for your comments!

past two years, preparing or updating the schedule should be the recommendation for the first priority. If the schedule exists, then you'll need to identify the most critical records management problem. Your survey data should help you make this decision.

Develop your program in stages. Every records manager I've ever known has had to struggle with limited staff and monetary resources. If you try to advance in too many areas at once, you'll be unsuccessful in all of them. Also, senior management tends to get nervous when they hear grandiose plans.

A better way is to present the overall strategy for the entire program in general terms, then identify the immediate priority and the benefits it will provide, and explain how you will accomplish that priority. By asking for approval on a step-by-step basis, you stand a much greater chance of getting it.

If management is still hesitant, I've found it helps to use the words "pilot program." Somehow, this doesn't sound as irrevocable, and it indicates you will be receptive to revaluation and modification of the program as needed.

I've also found it helpful to supplement the written action plan with some visual aids. For example, one records manager used photographs of the collapsing cartons in the company's records center to convince senior management to purchase shelving. Photographs of records stored in cardboard boxes in closets and stacked on top of overflowing cabinets in the office area also provide vivid testimony that a problem exists. Of course, if you take pictures of the records in a particular department, get the department head's permission in advance. Otherwise, the department head might feel you were trying to embarrass him or her as a poor manager.

In addition to photographs of problem areas, include illustrations of any new equipment to be purchased. Floor plans showing how much space will be opened up with the program provide further support. It also helps to include a "time line" or "milestone chart" indicating how long it will take to accomplish each step of the project and whose cooperation will be needed. In Chapter 4, I present the use of various project management tools, such as "milestone charts," in planning the program.

If you can get potential users of the program to comment on

the current records problems they face and how the program would benefit them, this will greatly strengthen your case.

If you don't gain immediate approval, don't give up. Instead, analyze the objections and develop appropriate responses or modify your proposal accordingly. For example, if the objection is cost, analyze the proposal to see where costs could be trimmed and what the ultimate effect would be. Perhaps less equipment could be installed initially, or the equipment could be leased.

Getting Cooperation From Users

Although upper management support is essential for implementing the program, you'll also need backing and cooperation from the program's users. Users can and do "sabotage" management approved programs when they perceive those programs as being unworthy of their support.

Just as you did with senior management, you'll need to determine the causes for any user resistance to records management. Usually the most basic cause is fear—the users' fear of losing control of their records or fear that a critical record will not be found when it's needed. I call this the "Linus syndrome." In the comic strip "Peanuts," Linus clings to his security blanket; most users feel the same way about their records.

Alleviating these fears is a matter of education and user involvement. As an initial step, have each department appoint a records coordinator. This individual will serve as a liaison between the records management group and the other members of his or her department. The coordinator should be someone who works well with others and has a good rapport with the rest of the department. The coordinator should also be receptive to new ideas, able to coordinate details well, and have been with the department for at least one year. It also helps if the coordinator is at least on the administrative assistant level or higher.

Although all managers need general information about the records management program, you'll work most closely with the department heads and the records coordinators. Department heads are responsible for making sure that you get full cooperation from their departments. To help ensure such support, it's a good idea to draft a memo for the signature of the president (or another top executive) that states why the records management program is being implemented and asks everyone involved to give you his or her full support. If you draft the memo, it's much more likely to say what you want and to be sent in a timely manner than if you just ask the executive to write it. Exhibit 2-3 is a sample of such a memo.

You'll find that your credibility with users increases gradually. If you can substantially help one department, word will spread and other departments will be more receptive to the program. It's also helpful to get the records management program featured in the company newsletter or magazine. Editors of such publications are usually looking for material, and "before and after" photographs are especially effective here. Of course, a good program is its own best marketing tool. Once people realize the benefits of the program, they'll support it.

An Ongoing Sales Effort

Promoting the records management program is not a one-time task. If records management is to be a success, effort must be applied steadily and consistently. The problem many organizations encounter is that after the initial push to get the program up and running, priorities shift. Funds and resources are cut; the program loses momentum and effectiveness. After several years of slipping, someone again recognizes that the organization has a "records problem," another major effort is begun, and the cycle starts over again.

If you have inherited a moribund program, first find out what caused the program to fade away. Then as you begin to resuscitate the program, stress why this version of the program is different and what steps you have taken to ensure the program's continued life.

It's the records manager's responsibility to ensure that the program remains a priority item and does not slip into oblivion. To achieve this goal, you must keep management aware of the program's accomplishments on an ongoing basis. You should also be

Exhibit 2-3. Memo From Senior Management

TO: All Department Heads

FROM: Emma Woodhouse, CEO

SUBJECT: Establishment of a Records Management Program

During the upcoming months, we will be establishing a records management program at Knightly, Inc. This program will:

- Ensure that we comply with all legal and regulatory record retention requirements
- Enable us to identify and protect those records that are essential to the corporation
- Improve the retrieval of records
- Allow us to develop strategies to manage the rapid growth of our records
- Conserve valuable office space through the off-site storage of inactive records and the destruction of duplicate and unnecessary records

Harriet Smith, Manager, Office Services, is responsible for establishing and maintaining the records management program. To ensure that the program meets your department's needs, I am asking you to appoint a records coordinator for your area.

While serving as coordinator will not require a major time commitment, it is a critical position. The coordinator will be your department's liaison in this area and will thus ensure that the program addresses the concerns of you and your staff. Therefore, the coordinator should have a good overall knowledge of your department's operation—possibly, the department's administrative assistant.

Initially we will ask the coordinators to gather some brief but essential information on the categories of records maintained in your area and your department's requirements for those records. Harriet will meet with the coordinators to explain exactly what information is needed and will provide guidance as needed during the process. This data will be used to prepare a records retention schedule for the company.

(continues)

Exhibit 2-3. *(continued)*

Please let Harriet know your choice for coordinator by [*date*]. Also, if you
have any questions about the program, please contact Harriet. I appreciate
your cooperation in this critical activity.

---

on the lookout for ways to expand the program and improve its
effectiveness.

One tool that helps maintain visibility is publishing a quarterly one-page newsletter that highlights some of the department's
accomplishments and discusses projects that are underway. Keep
the newsletter short, print it on colored paper to increase its visibility, and, above all, don't send it out by electronic mail (E-mail).
There is so much "junk" E-mail that many individuals ignore all
but the most urgent messages.

Also keep a "score sheet" during the year detailing the various ways you've saved the organization money and the amounts.
For example, if filing cabinet expenditures were reduced by 40 percent, indicate that fact and the dollar amount of the savings. Then,
when it's time to justify next year's budget, you'll be able to point
out how much your department has saved the company already.

Conducting training sessions for new employees helps maintain awareness. You also may want to hold periodic "open houses"
for various portions of the records management operation. For example, if you've opened a new central files area or installed a new
imaging system, have an open house when people can view the
facility and see how it works. One client of mine served cham-
pagne at the open house—I can assure you that does wonders for
attendance. However, even coffee and cookies will be an incentive.

Ongoing user cooperation is also essential. Users must be
aware that you will be responsive to their needs and interested in
improving the program whenever possible. When new department
heads and records coordinators are appointed, your group should
train them in the program instead of letting them assimilate it
gradually, and often incorrectly, on their own.

These continuous efforts make the company's initial investment in people, time, and money worthwhile and ensure the continued effectiveness of the program.

3

Developing and Staffing the Program

In the past, records management has been one of those functions for which few people wanted responsibility. As a result, many organizations abdicated responsibility altogether by stating that each department was responsible for developing and maintaining its own records management program. Other organizations assigned the responsibility to whoever did want it or placed it in the administrative services area (not necessarily a bad decision).

Today, organizations are more aware of the importance of their records. Also, document imaging technology has added some "sex appeal" to records management. Consequently, more thought is given to the decision on where to position records management, and more people are willing to take on the responsibility.

A Corporate Responsibility, but the Buck Stops Where?

As discussed in Chapter 2, it is critical that the records management function be centralized within the corporation. Expecting each department to develop expertise in this area is unrealistic. However, a large corporation may need to delegate responsibility to individual divisions or subsidiaries, specifying that they develop their own program within corporate guidelines and subject to corporate approval.

But which department should have overall accountability? That decision is no longer a simple one. As mentioned earlier, the traditional place for records management is in the administrative services area, along with such functions as reprographics, the mail room, facilities management, and office supplies. There is a certain logic to this approach because records management, like these other areas, is a support function that crosses departmental lines and provides service throughout the organization. Grouping these areas together increases the likelihood that users will receive efficient, comprehensive support services from a department that is accustomed to assisting others and perceives such assistance as its primary function.

However, in many organizations, the records management function has become increasingly automated. As a result, it is not uncommon to find records management as part of IS (information services or information systems) or MIS (management information systems). This grouping has the obvious advantage of giving the records management function direct access to strong technical support. A possible disadvantage is that paper is still a major component of most corporate record keeping, and systems personnel may be uncomfortable or unfamiliar with paper-based systems.

Whether or not records management is part of IS/MIS, the two areas must work closely together to ensure both the smooth implementation of computerized records management systems and the inclusion of electronic records in the overall records management program.

While records management is most commonly part of administrative services or IS/MIS, it may also be found under the auspices of legal, finance, the corporate secretary's office, or the library. In the past, I questioned the rationale behind these groupings. However, having seen records managers function successfully as a part of all of these areas, I've concluded that it's not where on the organization chart the function is, but the records manager's motivation and the support of top management that make the difference.

Staffing the Program—the Managerial Level

Once the basic idea of a central or corporate records management program has been accepted, staffing on both the managerial and clerical levels becomes a key issue.

On the managerial level, the first question is, "Do we need a full-time records manager?" Many smaller organizations (typically 500 employees or fewer) do function successfully with a records manager who has other duties as well. However, in these cases, the program is a relatively simple one, and the records manager has clerical support staff who also devote part of their time to the program. Larger organizations and any organization making an aggressive effort to reduce paper and increase control over records usually need a full-time records manager.

The next question is, "Where do you find a records manager?" While the number of records managers is increasing steadily, so is the number of companies needing records managers. However, if the company is willing to provide sufficient compensation, a qualified records manager can usually be "hired away" from another firm.

When bringing in someone from outside, the company may experience not only resistance to the records management concept, but also distrust of a newcomer. Consequently, the person brought in must have strong leadership qualities and the ability to "sell" the program, as well as professional competence in records management.

One way to locate such an individual is to advertise in either the ARMA (Association of Records Managers and Administrators) International newsletter or in newsletters of local ARMA chapters. Since ARMA is the professional organization of records managers, you can contact virtually all available qualified individuals at a relatively minimal cost. (ARMA International's address, as well as those of other related professional organizations, is given in the resource list at the end of this book.)

The other managerial alternative is to pick someone from within the organization and train him or her to handle the job. This approach can work extremely well. Unlike such fields as accounting and engineering, many highly qualified records managers have acquired most of their expertise "on the job."

Of course, the new records manager will need a concentrated training program through seminars and books such as this one. Also many colleges and universities are now offering courses in records management. Such courses can be a valuable resource, especially if taught by a practicing records manager or someone with extensive practical experience. It is, however, a good idea to check the faculty member's background, as courses are sometimes taught by individuals without "hands-on" experience.

It may also be helpful to hire a consultant to establish the program and "get it up and running." If you choose this approach, be sure that your staff has input in developing the program and acquires the expertise necessary to manage the program after the consultant's work is done.

Staffing—Clerical and First-Level Supervisory

Of course, records management programs require more than just managers. Depending on the scope of the program, you may need filing personnel, micrographics/document imaging equipment operators, data entry individuals, and records center staff. Since most of these positions primarily require on-the-job training, finding qualified personnel is relatively easy. Keeping them is another matter.

Several factors are responsible for the high turnover. One is low salaries; other types of work requiring comparable experience often pay better. Also, as individuals' skills improve, they may move on to better-paying positions. In addition to a low pay scale, the work is often monotonous and boring. Finally, these positions often receive little, if any, respect from others in the company. Remarks such as "Have the *girls* check the files" or "Have the *boy* get the box from the records center" are indicative of this problem.

The need to fill such positions is not going to go away. New technology has just changed the nature of the positions. Instead of more filing personnel, you may need more people doing data entry. Instead of more camera operators, you may need people to run document scanners. The jobs are changing, but they are still highly repetitive.

And although these jobs are routine, they are also essential and must be performed well. If there is continual turnover, you'll be constantly training new personnel—an expensive, time-consuming process. You'll also have to monitor quality control more closely.

But the situation is not hopeless. By adopting a combination of the following strategies, you can resolve these problems.

The first step is to upgrade both job titles and salaries. At the very least, your records personnel should receive pay comparable to that offered by other companies in the area for similar positions, and ideally the salaries should be greater.

In addition to increasing salaries, job titles should be upgraded and career paths created whenever possible. The two words I try to eliminate from job titles are "files" and "clerk." Both terms have negative connotations. Since we are no longer dealing with just paper, substitute "records" or "documentation" for "files." Alternatives for "clerk" are "specialist," "analyst," "coordinator," or "technician," depending on the exact nature of the position. Admittedly, you can't deposit a job title in the bank. But upgrading titles makes it easier to improve compensation, as well as helping to increase self-esteem.

Developing career paths relates closely to the enhanced job titles. One of the best tools for keeping qualified individuals is providing advancement opportunities within the records management area. For example, a new staff member might begin as a records analyst trainee and be promoted in three months to a records analyst if the filing systems are mastered. Then, nine months later, he or she could become a senior records analyst and acquire additional responsibilities. For this system to work, the titles should be linked to specific increases in responsibility as well as salary. And the career path should permit qualified individuals to move into supervisory positions when an appropriate opening occurs.

Upgrading positions and salaries does not solve the whole turnover problem. In most cases, you also need to make the jobs more interesting. A few people can file, scan, or do data entry quite happily all day, but most employees become bored, and the quality of their work suffers.

Two motivational approaches help reduce the monotony. The first is job enrichment—the technique of having one person perform several actions that comprise a complete process rather than the same action over and over. As a result, the individual assumes more control over and responsibility for his or her work. For example, in a manufacturing plant, a team of workers might build a major portion of the product, as opposed to individuals performing one specific function in the assembly-line method.

Job enrichment can be applied on a smaller scale in records management. For example, instead of having everyone file

throughout the file area, assign portions of the files to various employees and have them each assume responsibility for the maintenance of their files. This approach tends to increase the employees'
interest in their work, as they "learn" an area thoroughly. Filing is
done more carefully because employees know that they personally
will have to cope with any problems caused by their misfiles. And
when errors do occur, you can easily trace them to their source and
work with that employee to correct the problem.

Another technique to reduce boredom is cross-training—
teaching employees to perform more than one job. For example,
files personnel can learn how to prepare documents for scanning
or microfilming. This breaks the monotony of filing. Cross-training
personnel also means that you have trained backups available if
someone is on vacation or ill. One caution—some union situations
make it difficult or even impossible to cross-train employees.

As an additional motivational technique, some records managers have formed "quality teams" within their departments. Admittedly, this is primarily a tool for larger records management
departments, since at least four or five employees and a manager
or supervisor are needed for an effective quality team. The group
could be as large as ten employees and a manager.

The group should meet regularly—perhaps every two weeks
or once a month—to discuss ways to improve the department's
efficiency or resolve problems. The meeting should not be a
"bitch" session where everyone ventilates frustrations, but should
be directed toward solutions.

Emphasize that the group will look at both large and small
issues. Members should feel comfortable bringing up simple concepts like labeling file shelves differently, as well as complex issues
such as dealing with records center users who don't follow departmental procedures.

Since some people may initially feel reluctant to express their
ideas, it's a good idea to ask everyone to write down anonymously
two or three ideas for improving departmental operations or topics
for discussion and turn them in to the group leader. These ideas
can provide a good starting point for the discussion.

In addition to improving operations, quality teams also promote a sense of departmental unity. Individuals from one area,
such as filing, become familiar with the problems and issues faced

by other areas, such as microfilming or data entry, as well as learning how what they do affects others.

Also activities such as cross-training and quality teams help you identify qualified staff members who can move into supervisory positions. Promoting from within shows that career paths really do exist.

Alternative Sources of Personnel

Having read this far, some records managers might say, "My problem isn't turnover; I don't have any staff to turn over. How do I get approval to add staff?" At many companies, the standard response to the request for staff is, "We don't want to add head count." And the records manager understandably feels frustrated when he or she has prepared five pages of carefully worded justification explaining exactly what the new person will do and why the position is essential, only to be told "no new FTEs" (full-time employees).

Now it's time to drop back and punt. If you can't get full-time staff, consider part-time personnel. Part-time staff is often easier to justify since the company usually does not have to pay benefits and can terminate them easily if costs have to be cut. One viable alternative is to hire retired individuals to work a limited number of hours. These individuals might be former employees, or you might recruit at a local senior citizens' center. Many retired individuals want to supplement their income and are very conscientious, highly motivated staff members.

Also consider individuals who would like to work part time while their children are in school. High school work-study programs are another possibility, especially for routine, repetitive tasks which become tedious if done for eight hours a day. And finally, if a local college or university offers courses in records management, consider sponsoring an internship. The student works part time and writes a paper based on the experience gained on the job.

Temporary agencies are another source of personnel. Quite frankly, I'm ambivalent on this one. Some of my clients have found outstanding staff members this way. On the other hand, by the time you get the temporary trained, he or she may have moved on to another job or left the agency. You also have to be sure the person has adequate skills. Unfortunately, not all agencies screen employees carefully, and literacy is not something you can take for granted, so check any new individual's work carefully.

One other source of personnel—both full and part time—deserves mention. Consider hiring physically or mentally disabled individuals for some positions. Individuals who are hearing impaired or unable to walk can operate a scanner or perform data entry with no difficulty. Preparing documents for imaging and certain types of routine filing are tasks that some mentally disabled persons can handle very well.

Since there are affirmative action programs for hiring disabled individuals, your human resources department should be able to assist you in finding qualified candidates. Shelter workshops and social agencies are also a good source of referrals. Some of these groups even operate microfilming service bureaus and can provide trained micrographics personnel.

Of course, qualified individuals with disabilities should move upward along the records management career path in the same way other department members do.

One last comment on personnel—whatever the job title or pay scale, your employees should be treated with respect and courtesy, both by you and by others in the company with whom they interact. It's your responsibility to establish a precedent here, by referring to employees by their name or job title, not as the "girls" or the "boys," and by making sure that others within the company treat your staff with similar courtesy.

Professional Staff Development

Records management is a rapidly changing field, particularly in the technological area. As a result, both records managers and their staff need to devote considerable time and effort to professional growth and development. Membership in ARMA International is an excellent first step. For a modest annual fee, members receive the *Records Management Quarterly,* as well as newsletters and chapter publications. For a nominal extra charge, members can join an Industry Action Committee (IAC) comprised of records managers in specific industries such as pharmaceuticals, utilities, state government, banking/financial services, and so on. Of course, the most valuable aspect of membership is the opportunity to meet and exchange ideas with others in the same profession through local chapter meetings and regional and national events.

The resource list at the end of this book also lists a number of other professional organizations of value to the records manager such as AIIM (Association for Information and Image Management), NIRMA (Nuclear Information and Records Management Association), and OASI (Office Automation Society International).

Like many other professions, records management has a certification program, in this case sponsored by the Institute of Certified Records Managers. To become a certified records manager (CRM), you must have a degree from a four-year accredited college and a minimum of three years of full-time professional experience in records management. Or, if you have three years of college, you will need five years of records management experience. With a two-year associate degree, seven years' experience is required, and if you have no college, eleven years' experience will be needed. You must also pass a series of examinations on the various aspects of records management.

4

Using Project Management Tools to Plan and Control the Program

While records management is an ongoing process, setting up each phase of the program is a specific project. When that phase of the program is operational, you have completed that project and are now in the "maintenance mode." In other words, projects are designed to accomplish a specific objective. They have a beginning and an end.

Projects need to be planned carefully and then to be monitored against the plan. The extent of the planning depends on the complexity of the project. For a relatively simple project such as organizing a training session for new records coordinators, you would probably just jot down all the things you need to do on a "to do" list and check them off as they're completed.

However, very few records management projects fall under the category of "relatively simple." The projects often take months to accomplish and involve multiple individuals and considerable sums of money. If you don't have a "game plan" for managing the project, you can easily find yourself embarrassed by missed deadlines or overlooked details. Project management is simply a method and set of techniques for managing the project from start to finish.

This chapter deals with project management from a mid-level approach, which is about where most records management projects fall on a scale of complexity. After all, we're not building a skyscraper; on the other hand, we're doing something considerably more complex than planning a departmental Christmas party.

Defining Your Objective

The first step is determining what you want to accomplish. The project's objective or goal should be specific, measurable, and realistic. It should also include a time frame. Samples of well-defined records management project goals are:

- Prepare a records retention schedule for the corporate headquarters by August 1, 1996.
- Index all inactive records currently in storage by October 1, 1996.

A poorly defined project goal would be:

- Establish a corporate records management program.

The problem here is that we haven't defined what we mean by a "records management program" or set a deadline for the project.

While the well-defined goals include a deadline, in many cases you won't know what that deadline will be until you progress further in the planning process. Thus, unless you have a deadline set by upper management, the time frame may need to be added near the end of the planning process.

Identifying the Activities

Any project is a sequence of activities. Each activity is a measurable, manageable step in the overall process. For example, if your goal was to identify a commercial records center to use for storing inactive records, some of the activities might be:

- Identifying the records storage centers in your area that could meet your needs
- Preparing a request for proposal (RFP)
- Reviewing the responses to the RFP and selecting final candidates
- Negotiating terms with the final candidates
- Deciding which center you'll use

In some cases, you may want to use a two-tiered approach, first listing all the major activities and then dividing each into the various tasks that must be performed to accomplish the activity. In the preceding list, preparing the RFP might include these tasks:

- Drafting the RFP
- Having purchasing review the RFP
- Having your boss review and approve the RFP

Sequencing the Activities

The next step is organizing the activities in the order in which they must be performed. While you can diagram the steps or enter them into a project management software package, I prefer to start by writing each task on an individual self-adhesive note, such as 3-M's "Post-its." Next you take a large sheet of paper and arrange the steps in a logical pattern. After the pattern is set, then you use a pencil to connect the steps together.

Be sure to indicate when steps can be performed concurrently and which steps must be completed before others can commence. The self-sticking notes allow you to move steps around until you reach the most logical sequence. This is also an excellent interactive approach to use when a team is blocking out the steps in a project. Take your time and make sure the steps are properly ordered.

Exhibit 4-1 is a sample project sequence diagram. Such a sequence is sometimes called a PERT (Program Evaluation and Review Technique) chart. Note the arrows connecting the activities and showing the work flow. Note, too, the start and end symbols. Each task must connect to another activity or to the start or end symbols. You don't want any loose ends!

Determining the Time Frame

The next step is assigning times to each activity. You'll notice that has been done in Exhibit 4-1. You can use either days or weeks for the time frame but be consistent. If your job involves more than

Exhibit 4-1. Sample Project Sequence Diagram With Critical Path

Project: Preparing a Records Retention Schedule

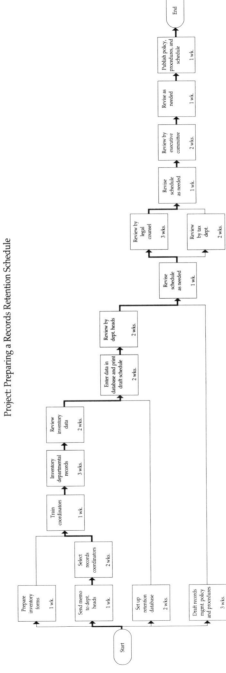

Critical path — (22 weeks)

Note: This example covers only the preparation of a retention schedule, not the implementation. Actual time required to perform various tasks varies from organization to organization.

just completing the project, I would use weeks as you'll have to perform other duties while accomplishing the project tasks. With such a schedule, days usually become unrealistic.

When you calculate the times, remember that you're not listing the time to actually do the task but the time that will elapse before the task is completed. For example, it might only take you two hours to write a memo, but that task will need to be "sandwiched" in between other activities. Hence, you might allow two days or even one week for it on the project sequence. Also once you actually match the project to the calendar, you may have to allow additional time for holidays, vacations, and the like.

For steps that will be performed by other individuals, get them to provide a time estimate—don't guess how long you think it will take them. Having them supply an estimate also helps strengthen their commitment to the project. Confirm any verbal time commitments by sending them a copy of the diagram with a note that you've factored in their time estimates.

After you've assigned time periods to each task, the next step is determining the critical path. This is the longest path in the project sequence from start to finish. Hence, it is the minimum time that you will require to complete the project. In Exhibit 4-1, the critical path is the bold line (twenty-two weeks).

In addition to telling you how long it will take to complete the project, the critical path also tells you where you have some slack or flex. For example, we've estimated three weeks for drafting the records management policy and procedures. However, you actually have thirteen weeks before the material is required. You can be behind schedule here for up to ten weeks without affecting the overall project's deadline. But don't get too comfortable or put everything off until the last minute—you might be surprised then by an unexpected crisis.

Preparing a Milestone Chart

While the project sequence and critical path are excellent tools for organizing the project, you'll probably want to prepare a milestone chart (also called a Gantt chart) to communicate the schedule to others and to use as a project control tool. The milestone chart shows clearly the time you expect each step in the project to take. Exhibit 4-2 is a milestone chart for the project diagrammed in Exhibit 4-1.

There are a number of different formats for milestone charts. I find the format shown in Exhibit 4-2 easy to use and understand. If you are planning the project in days instead of weeks, then each large column would be a week and would have five narrow columns under it for the days of the week.

Activities are shown as follows:

Estimated time for a task:	—————— △
Task completed on schedule:	—————— ▲
Task rescheduled:	————— △ ———— ☐
Task rescheduled and completed:	————— △ ———— ◼

The darkened line and triangle indicate the project was completed on schedule. Extending the line and adding a square indicates rescheduling. Darkening the square indicates completion in accordance with the rescheduling. If the task needs to be rescheduled again, you would again extend the line and add another square.

As Exhibit 4-2 shows, tasks 1, 2, 5, and 6 were completed on schedule, while tasks 3 and 4 had to be rescheduled. Fortunately neither of these tasks was on the critical path. Hence rescheduling them has not delayed the overall schedule. Task 3 has been completed, but task 4 is still unfinished.

When you're initially doing the milestone chart, use a pencil because you may find yourself revising it as you go along. It's also a good idea to leave a blank line between every task. Then if you do have to add in an item, you can easily do so.

While I strongly recommend project sequences and critical paths for any major project, you may find the milestone chart alone adequate for minor projects (usually ten or fewer activities). Also "generic" milestone charts are helpful for projects that are repeated, such as the annual revision of the retention schedule. With a generic chart, you'd head your large columns "month 1," "month 2," etc., or "week 1," "week 2," etc.

Exhibit 4-2. Sample Milestone Chart (end of month 1)

PROJECT									DATE	PAGE
Preparation of Records Retention Schedule for Knightley, Inc.									8/20/95	1 of 1

TASK	DESCRIPTION	PERFORMED BY	SEPT.	OCT.	NOV.	DEC.	JAN.	FEB.
1	Send memo to department heads	CEO/Rec. Mgr.	◀					
2	Prepare inventory form	Rec. Mgr.	◀					
3	Set up retention database	Rec. Mgr./ Systems Support	▲					
4	Draft R.M. policy and procedures	Rec. Mgr.	△	□				
5	Select records coordinators	Dept. Heads	◢					
6	Train records coordinators	Rec. Mgr.	▲					
7	Inventory departmental records	Rec. Coords.		△				
8	Review inventory data	Rec. Mgr.			△			
9	Enter data in database & print schedule	Rec Asst.			△			
10	Review schedule (dept. heads)	Dept. Heads				△		
11	Revise schedule as needed	Rec. Mgr./ Rec. Asst.				△		
12	Review by legal counsel	General Counsel					△	
13	Review for tax issues	Head, Tax Dept.					△	
14	Revise schedule as needed	Rec. Mgr./ Rec. Asst.					△	
15	Review by executive committee	Exec. Comm.					△	
16	Revise schedule as needed	Rec. Mgr./ Rec. Asst.					△	
17	Publish policy, procedure, & schedule	Rec. Mgr./Rec. Asst., Print Shop						△

Using the Milestone Chart as a Communications Tool

While project sequences and milestone charts both help you "get your act together," the milestone chart is also an excellent communication tool.

When you are presenting the project to management for approval, it's an excellent idea to include the milestone chart. This shows that you have planned the project carefully and thought out the details. It also shows whose involvement is needed to make the project a success.

Finally, it defuses a common problem encountered by records managers—unrealistic time expectations. I always begin my seminars by asking participants to introduce themselves and state their objectives in attending the class. Almost invariably, someone explains that he or she is there to prepare a retention schedule and the deadline is two to four weeks from today. Now, if you're new to records management, you might not realize that this is a totally absurd deadline—but, trust me, it is.

But how does the records manager communicate the absurdity of the deadline without appearing lazy or disorganized? The milestone chart is the answer. It clearly shows why the project takes as long as it does. Also, it can be used as a negotiating tool. If management insists that the project be done more quickly, the records manager can point out what additional resources (time and money) are needed to reduce the time shown to complete the various tasks.

Often a team is organized to establish the records management program. In these situations, the milestone chart becomes an excellent communications tool for the team members. I like to post a large milestone chart on the wall where everyone can see it. The chart shows clearly what progress has been made and what, if any, steps are behind schedule. And sometimes, the "shame factor" helps with individuals who don't have a sense of urgency about deadlines.

You can also use the chart as a management reporting device. Simply submit it monthly with a short explanation for any tasks that are behind schedule.

Monitoring Project Performance

After the project is underway, use the milestone chart to monitor performance. At the end of each week, review the milestone charts for the projects you're working on. (Hopefully, you'll use this tool for *all* major projects, not just those dealing with records management.) See where you're on schedule and where you need to take action to catch up.

At the company for which I used to work, employees had to submit milestone charts each month to the individuals they reported to along with a brief explanation of what was behind schedule and why. I very quickly got into the habit of checking my charts at the end of the third week of the month and making sure I'd got everything back on schedule by the fourth week.

Now it's time for some reality. Projects, especially records management projects, are rarely completed on schedule. Sometimes, of course, the problem is poor planning. But often, the problem is factors beyond the manager's control. As we've discussed already, many records managers wear multiple hats. Just when the project is well underway, the manager may be told to shift priorities and concentrate his or her efforts on extinguishing the current fire. The records management project then is put "on hold."

When this happens, let me encourage you to try to make at least some progress on the records management project. Even if it's not all that you had hoped for, anything that moves the project forward is beneficial. In my almost twenty years as a consultant, I've seen a great deal of time, money, and energy thrown away on projects that were begun but not completed. If the project is still worth doing, keep it going somehow. Otherwise, you and the project lose credibility.

In such situations, it helps to be forthright in your communications. Explain to everyone affected why the project has been rescheduled, prepare a revised milestone chart or schedule, and indicate what steps will take place in the interim to keep the project moving forward.

Learning More About Project Management

One chapter can only provide a brief introduction to project management. What I've included here are the two project management tools that I use most frequently: the project sequence diagram with critical path and the milestone chart. I use these techniques on virtually every project I manage, and I've found them to be invaluable. And, for many records managers, these two tools will meet your needs.

However, if you find yourself managing extremely large and complex projects, you may want to learn more about project management. I've included some excellent books on the subject in the bibliography. Also the American Management Association offers a number of fine seminars on project management.

Another resource is project management software. Such software prepares work breakdown structures (an interim scheduling step I omitted here), project sequence diagrams, milestone charts, and so on, and allows you to change these documents very easily. Two extremely popular PC packages are Scitor's "Project Scheduler" and "Microsoft Project for Windows." If you're only going to use the tools once or twice a year, you'll probably spend more time learning the software than you would diagramming the charts. But if you're managing a number of projects, you'll find the software a valuable tool.

5

Records Retention
Part I: Conducting the Records Inventory

After considering where records management belongs in the organization, the proper staffing of the department, and planning the project, you're probably wondering, "Where do I start?" Of course, you can't institute the entire program at once. The exact order of the steps you choose depends on the current status of records management within the organization.

However, if you don't have a records retention schedule or if the schedule you have has not been revised within the past two years, records retention is a logical first step. Implementing a retention schedule enables you to destroy all unnecessary records. Once you've cleared out the deadwood, it's much easier to organize what's left and select appropriate storage and retrieval procedures. In fact, for that reason, records retention is sometimes referred to as records "disposition."

Another reason for beginning here is that retention includes inventorying all of the organization's records. And until you know what you have, it's impossible to formulate the rest of the program.

A third reason for making the retention schedule a high priority is that it demonstrates compliance with the legal retention requirements established by federal, state, and local government. By implementing a consistent legal program for disposing of records, the company shows that it is not destroying records selectively to conceal evidence. This can be a critical issue if the company is involved in litigation.

The Five Steps

Successfully implementing records retention is a five step process. The steps are:

1. Inventorying the records
2. Determining how long to keep them
3. Preparing the schedule
4. Obtaining approval for the schedule
5. Implementing the schedule

The remainder of this chapter deals with the first and biggest step—inventorying the records, while the next chapter covers the remaining steps.

The Rationale Behind the Inventory

The records inventory determines what records the organization has, where they are located, and how many of them there are. You *cannot* conduct a successful inventory by sending out questionnaires to department heads. Even if they do complete the questionnaires, they are likely to forget to include some record categories or not supply the necessary level of detail. I'll always remember the form submitted by one department head that listed the record title as "binders" and requested a five year retention with no indication as to what, if anything, was in the binders.

To get meaningful information, you need to have a physical inventory conducted by properly trained individuals. But before you panic utterly, murmuring "That could take years," let's consider what your goal is. It's not to identify every piece of paper stored in the company or even every different type of document. Instead, it's to identify records *categories* or what's known in records management jargon as "records series."

For example, the paid invoices in accounts payable would be one category. The invoice file might include not only the invoice, but also the purchase requisition, purchase order, receiving report, and check copy. However, because these records are filed together and treated as a unit, they are one category and would require one inventory form. Another example of a category would be employee personnel files. Again the file would contain a number of different documents—the application, resume, performance appraisals, notices of promotions, and so on—but the file itself is a single category. Other record categories, of course, might contain only one type of document, such as "canceled checks" or "employment applications for non-hires."

In addition to the concept of record categories, you need to remember our definition of a record (Chapter 1). In other words, you are not only inventorying paper in file folders, but also computer printouts, microfilm, magnetic media, photographs, slides, engineering drawings—in short, any *recorded* information.

Although I've stressed the idea of a comprehensive records inventory, there is one exception. If the company has a number of branch locations or field offices performing the same basic functions and keeping similar records, you need only inventory the records at one or two representative locations.

Collecting the Data

Since one of the goals of records managers is to reduce paper, you may want to consider doing a paperless inventory. By this I mean entering the data directly into the computer, instead of using a form. This is a definite possibility if you have access to a laptop computer and if you and/or your staff are doing the inventory. The sooner you can enter the data in a computer, the sooner you can massage and manipulate it.

Another paperless alternative is to dictate the data into a portable recorder and then have it transcribed directly into the computer. (Chapter 6 will discuss fields for the retention database and its use.)

However, if you're having the records coordinators collect the data—an option discussed later in this chapter, use forms. It'll be simpler, and you won't have to "clean up" or delete any inaccurate or unnecessary information that may have been entered in the database.

Whether you input data directly into the computer or use a form, you will need to collect certain information about each record category. Exhibit 5-1 is an example of a records inventory form. If you wish, you may reproduce this form (and all others in this book) for your own use. Or you may prefer to modify the form to fit your organization's special needs.

Completing the Inventory Form

A review of the inventory items in Exhibit 5-1 will indicate the type of information you should collect. It's a good idea to obtain both the department name and number (usually the accounting code assigned to that department). It will be simpler to organize the schedule by department number, but the name will remind you of the department's actual function.

In some cases, the title of the record will be obvious—purchase orders, for example. In other cases, the title may need clarification. For example, five departments may have "project files," each containing different types of information and referring to different types of projects. More appropriate titles might be "plant maintenance project files" or "telecommunications project files."

Avoid informal names for record titles or organizational slang. I once received an inventory form with the record title "adds and kills." No, the company wasn't into gang warfare; this was their name for the "membership addition and deletion report." Since corporate legal counsel might have to present the schedule in court, you should use clear, descriptive titles that don't cause confusion.

If more than one department keeps copies of the record, be sure the same title is used consistently. For example, different departments might refer to the same report as "monthly budget reports," "summary budget reports," and "budget summaries." An appropriate standard title would be "Budget reports—departmental—monthly." A separate inventory form should be prepared for each department that has a copy of the record.

After you've established the title, the next step is determining whether you are inventorying the *copy of record* or a duplicate copy. The copy of record is the organization's "official" copy. When this copy is no longer needed in the office, it will be placed in inactive storage at the company's records center for the remainder of its life span. Duplicates, however, are only kept in the office for as long as they are needed and then destroyed.

The next question, of course, is "How do you determine which

Exhibit 5-1. Sample Records Inventory Form

RECORDS INVENTORY	
Dept. Name	Dept. No.

Record Title

☐ original or "official" copy of record   ☐ duplicate

For forms and computer printouts, form or report no.: _____

Description of record and any other comments: _____

_____

_____

_____

Filing equipment type: _____ Filing method:

☐ alphabetic ☐ numeric ☐ date ☐ other: _____

Year	Volume	Activity Level

Media: ☐ paper ☐ microfilm/microfiche ☐ other: _____

Administrative retention (indicate the number of years on the appropriate lines): _____ in office _____ in storage

Others with copies of record (if known): _____

Inventoried by: _____ Date: _____

===

To be completed by records management department:

Legal retention: _____

Comments: _____

_____

_____

_____

Final retention decision: _____ yrs. in office _____ yrs. in storage

Approved by: _____ Date: _____

copy is the copy of record?" There is no one answer that always works, but the following guidelines will resolve the issue:

- If the original is kept within the company, it normally becomes the copy of record.
- If the original is not kept within the company (a letter, for example), then the originator's copy becomes the copy of record.
- If neither of the above conditions is met, then the copy of record is the copy belonging to the department that has the greatest need and use for the record or the complete set. For example, the legal department would have the copy of record for "litigation files," and the accounts payable department would have the copy of record for "paid invoices."

Distinguishing between the copy of record and duplicates is essential to ensure that one and only one copy is kept for an extended period. Not only do duplicates waste valuable space, but they can cause legal problems. Often, in litigation, the other side will request that all copies of a record in existence be produced. This is done in hopes of finding an incriminating note on one of the copies. Even if your personnel have properly refrained from writing such notes, the mere cost of finding and producing all copies can add substantially to litigation expense. It's much simpler and cheaper if you can show that the retention schedule called for the destruction of duplicates after six months or one year and that the policy was followed.

The next items on the form provide added clarification. The form or report number, when one exists, ensures that everyone is referring to the same record. The description might include a listing of the different types of documents in the file, a brief explanation of how the record is used, and any other pertinent comments.

The information on filing equipment type and method is primarily of value later in helping departments improve filing practices.

The next section of the form is critical. For each year, you want to find out how much of the record exists and how frequently it is used. Breaking these items down by year lets you determine if the record category is high volume and growing rapidly. In such cases, it may be desirable to convert the record to another medium. Also, if older years are referenced infrequently, they should be sent to off-site storage. Likewise, records that occupy a great deal of space should be sent to storage as soon as possible, while it may be more practical to keep low volume records in the office.

Volume can be measured in several ways. The simplest is to indicate the number of file drawers (i.e., 3 ½ 36-inch drawers). Another alternative is to measure filing inches or feet (3 ½ 36-inch drawers would be 10 ½ feet).

The activity level might be daily, weekly, monthly, quarterly, rarely, or never. Asking by year helps clarify at what point the use of the records drops off significantly (usually after the first or second year). It's a good idea to discuss activity levels with support staff, as well as with managers. I've had some managers swear that they are using certain files every day. Then I've talked to their administrative assistants who say they've never seen the drawer opened or even, in one case, that the drawer was broken and couldn't be opened!

The medium is important because a record may exist in more than one form (both paper and microfilm, for example). You'll want to indicate in the schedule how long each form should be kept.

The administrative retention is how many years the department head wants to keep the record in the office and, if it should go to storage, how many years there. You'll use this information in setting the retention value (see Chapter 6).

Listing other departments known to have copies of the record makes it easier to determine which copy should be the copy of record and also ensures that all departments' retention needs are considered.

The remaining portion of the form will be completed by the records management department as part of the process for determining how long the record should be kept.

Who Should Perform the Inventory

As you've probably guessed by now, inventorying is the most labor-intensive step in preparing the retention schedule. It's also a step you want to complete as quickly as possible. The inventory is equivalent to a photograph of the records, and the more time that elapses, the more things change.

Several alternatives exist for performing the inventory. One, obviously, is for the records manager and his or her staff to do it. If there is enough staff support and the organization is not too large, this may be a viable option. It does ensure high quality data, and the records management team learns a great deal about the records.

However, many records managers have other duties besides records management and have minimal support staff. In these cases, sharing the responsibility may be the best alternative. Having each department's records coordinator inventory his or her area expedites the process and ensures that no one person has a large amount to inventory.

If you elect this alternative, you are going to need to train the coordinators carefully. They are going to need to understand each of the items on the form. It usually helps to begin with a group training session where you go over the reasons for preparing the schedule and the inventory form, followed by one-on-one sessions with each individual coordinator in his or her work area. The one-on-one sessions are especially helpful as individuals can show you specific record categories about which they have questions. Also, a coordinator may not feel comfortable discussing specific departmental situations in a training session with other departments present.

The down side to using coordinators is that some individuals may not complete the forms carefully. You'll have to do a certain amount of follow-up to collect all of the data and to resolve inconsistencies or unclear information. However, this method takes less of your time than doing it yourself, and it does get departments involved in the process.

Still another alternative is to have a consultant do the inventorying. Since the consultant has done this many times before, he or she can usually collect the data more quickly than you would. While departments have to spend some time with the consultant, this method requires less effort on their part. Of course, using a consultant increases costs.

Tips on Inventorying

Whichever approach you elect, departments should receive advance notification of the inventory and the reasons for it. The inventories should be scheduled at times that are convenient for the various departments. (But don't accept the excuse that no time is convenient.) Be sure that both the department heads and the secretaries or others responsible for file maintenance will be in the office during the inventory. Then if there is a question about a particular record category, a qualified individual will be present to answer it.

If the inventorying is not being done by a department member, it should be done in the presence of such a person. This practice prevents misunderstanding and ensures that the person doing the inventory is not accused of misplacing or removing records.

Persistence is often necessary to ensure that *all* of the department's records are located. Records don't just reside in file cabinets. They may be found in closets, cartons, storage cabinets, bookcases, and, of course, people's desks. Obviously, you can't go through someone's desk without their permission. But you can ask them to show you whatever records they maintain in the desk; feel free to ignore the back issues of *Playboy* or *Cosmopolitan* and other items of a personal nature. Beware, however, of employees who tell you all their records are "personal." If it's work they did for the organization, it's not personal and it should be inventoried.

"Subject" or "Administrative" Files

In virtually every department, you'll find what may be called a "subject," "administrative," "miscellaneous" or "A to Z" file. This file is an alphabetical collection of "administrivia"—mainly duplicate information or items no one knew where to file, but didn't want to destroy. Assigning each file a separate retention is a lost cause, especially since new files may be created daily.

What I usually do is ask appropriate department personnel if there are any files they wish to keep longer than two years. If so, these should be assigned a proper retention period and listed separately in the schedule. Ideally important records should not be stored in a general or miscellaneous file where they might accidentally be lost or thrown away. One firm actually threw away its articles of incorporation during a purge of a "miscellaneous" file!

The remaining files can be listed on the retention schedule as "departmental subject files" or "departmental administration files." The retention should not exceed two years, and the files should not go to storage. One way to ensure that these files don't grow out of proportion is to limit the amount of filing space available for them (usually one to two drawers). It also helps to set up new folders for each topic each year. This process makes it easy to identify and destroy files that are over two years old.

Inventorying Computer-Readable Media

Inventorying paper or microfilm files is relatively simple as you can view the record and determine its contents. However, records kept on a computer present a special challenge.

Let's begin with the computer files maintained by the corporate systems department. There may already be a tape retention schedule listing all the tapes in existence and the retention for each. In this case, your task is simply verifying the appropriateness of the retentions. However, most of the time I find that the issue has not been addressed, and the backup tapes are being kept "indefinitely" or "forever."

There are two basic issues with tape retention. One is disaster recovery—how much backup material does the systems staff need to recreate the system in case of a disaster? Clearly they must be the judges of this issue.

The other issue is the users' need for old data. How many years back do users need to access the information? If certain information does need to be kept for longer periods than the system backup requirements, it is desirable to store that information separately and possibly on a more durable medium than magnetic tapes—such as CD-ROM or optical disks.

Unlike paper files, tapes cannot simply be tossed in a box, stored for many years, and then pulled out and reused. The tapes need to be stored in a climate-controlled facility. If a retention of several years is needed, the tapes may need to be rewound or copied at certain intervals to ensure that they remain readable. These are all issues that should be discussed with the systems staff.

And, of course, any computer medium is useless unless there is equipment to run it on. I often find companies storing old tapes from earlier computer systems—tapes for which they no longer have the necessary equipment or software. Reviewing tape retentions and adjusting them can save significant amounts of storage costs since tapes are usually stored at commercial facilities. One firm saved over $15,000 a year by reducing its off-site backup tape retention from six years to four years.

Also, should litigation occur, backup media may have to be searched for pertinent information. In addition to being costly, such a search may reveal information that is not in the organization's best interests.

Inventorying the systems group's computer files can be accomplished by working directly with that area. However, you have only viewed the tip of the iceberg. Most organizations have a large complement of personal computers, loaded with various files.

Two issues arise in connection with PC files. One is establishing retentions for critical files. The other is protecting them from accidental destruction. Keep in mind that there is no way you can inventory all files users create. But you can and should identify critical files of long-term importance to the organization.

The best way to identify the files is to have each of the system users complete a form similar to the one in Exhibit 5-2 for each major file they have.

Identifying these files is important, not just to set retentions, but because the organization needs to know what information it has. We've always known what files are on the main computer systems. But in this age of client-server systems and decentralized computing, most data is being created by individuals. If an individual leaves the organization or is unexpectedly taken ill, this knowledge can be difficult or even impossible to locate. With paper files you can at least browse through the folders, but searching innumerable PC directories for specific records is time consuming and frustrating. Having a list of critical files can save a great deal of time in an emergency.

If the computers are part of a LAN (local area network), files on the network are normally protected by a system backup. However, not all computers are on networks, and even with networked systems, some users prefer to store certain files on the hard drive

Exhibit 5-2. Records Inventory Form for Individual User and Small System Computer Readable Media

---

Please complete a form for each personal computer file that is of long-term importance to your department and/or that is updated regularly or used for an extended period. You do not need to inventory any files that are on a mainframe or data center system.

Dept. Name	Dept. No.
Your Name	Date

File Title on Computer System

Brief Description of File Contents and Purpose: _____

_____

_____

_____

How often is file updated?
☐ Daily   ☐ Weekly   ☐ Monthly   ☐ Never
☐ Other: _____

Where is the file stored?
☐ Network   ☐ Hard drive   ☐ Diskette

If the file is kept on a hard drive or diskette, how often is it backed up?
☐ Daily   ☐ Weekly   ☐ Monthly   ☐ Never
☐ Other: _____

Is a backup copy maintained off-site?   ☐ Yes   ☐ No

If yes, where is off-site copy located?   _____

Is a hard copy of the file kept also?   ☐ Yes   ☐ No

If yes, where is/are the hard copy/copies kept?
☐ In our department   ☐ Other: _____

or on diskette. And many of these users do not back up their files regularly. Even if they do, the backup is usually stored next to the PC, so that the same disaster, a fire, for example, can destroy both. Backups of all critical files should be kept off-site.

Since inventorying computer-readable media is a major project in and of itself, you may want to divide the records retention process into two phases. Phase I would be preparing the retention schedule for paper and microfilm records, while Phase II would address electronic media. Other records managers choose to tackle the entire project at once.

Whichever approach you elect, do not ignore computer-readable files. These are just as much company records as paper files. While space savings is not as much of an issue with them, they may be subpoenaed and, in some cases, there are legal requirements as to their retention. And, of course, they are a valuable asset, representing many hours of individuals' time.

What Next?

Performing the inventory is the most labor-intensive part of the retention process. So when you've done this, you've fought half the battle. The next steps, addressed in Chapter 6, are determining how long to keep the records and preparing and implementing the schedule.

6

Records Retention
Part II: Preparing and Implementing the Schedule

Records Appraisal

After the inventory is complete, the records must be appraised—not for their monetary worth, but for their value to the organization and, in particular, for the length of time they should be kept. As part of the appraisal process, four types of value must be considered for each record. They are:

1. Administrative or operational value
2. Legal value
3. Fiscal/tax value
4. Historical or archival value

Let's examine each value separately to see how it is determined and who determines it.

Administrative Value

The administrative value is the length of time the record may be needed or used within the company. This value is usually set by the department head who is responsible for the copy of record, although the needs of other departments using the record should also be considered.

In addition to an overall retention value, the department head should also set a period of active use. For this period, the record will be kept in the office; then, it will go to the records center for the remainder of the retention period. For most records, the active period should not exceed two years, and it may be substantially less. Of course, there are exceptions, such as an employee's personnel file, which remains active as long as the employee is with the company.

Many managers are unsure as to what administrative period to request. If you encounter this, a good way to approach the issue is "How many years back have you ever referred to this record? Three years? Six years? Why did you refer to the record? How important was it that you had the record?"

A few managers feel all of their records should be permanent. "Permanent" is a designation that should be used on a very limited basis. In most cases, I argue strongly for a specific time period, even if it is a relatively long one such as twenty-five or even fifty years.

If the schedule is being done for the first time, give managers some latitude here because you want them to get used to the concept of disposing of records. However, keep track of record categories where you suspect the retentions are excessive and monitor the retrievals of the older records. (This can be done through computerized indexing of the records in the records center. See Chapter 7.) Then, a year later when the schedule is up for revision, you can negotiate for shorter retentions, pointing out that the older records have not been accessed.

Legal Value

How long the company needs a record is one issue. How long the government thinks you should keep it is another. There are over 10,000 federal statutes and regulations governing records retention, plus a variety of state and local requirements. And no government or court will accept ignorance of a regulation as a satisfactory excuse for noncompliance.

Some organizations simply adopt a "suggested" or "recommended" retention schedule that has been prepared by a vendor or consultant for general use. While such schedules may serve as guidelines, you don't want to follow them blindly because different types of companies are accountable to different regulatory agencies. As a result, two companies may have different retention requirements for the same record. Also, state and local requirements vary widely, and the company must comply with the retention requirements for the states in which it has business operations.

As a further complication, government agencies set their retention requirements autonomously. That is, for the same record, one agency may specify a three year period, another six years, and a third may simply say "maintain the record." Normally you have to comply with the longest period set by the agencies that regulate your organization. "Maintain the record" may be taken to mean the administrative value or a three year retention period, whichever is longer.

This may all sound so overwhelming that your reaction is "Let's keep everything forever. Then we're sure to be in compliance." That's true, but this is a very costly form of compliance. First, there is the expense of storing the records. Second, if the company is sued, it will be required to produce *everything* it has relating to the suit. And if everything's been kept, the cost of finding and reproducing all appropriate documents may be substantial. Third, the records you produce may not always be in your best interests. An old document may contain information damaging to the company's case. If you were not required to keep the document and destroyed it in compliance with your retention policy, you're protected. But if you do have it, you have to produce it.

Also keep in mind that all 10,000 regulations do not affect any one organization. For example, you might find a statute on retention requirements for employment records kept in a coal mining apprenticeship program. Unless your industry is coal mining, this requirement is totally irrelevant. Your concern is with the requirements that affect your business.

Resources for Determining Legal Retention Requirements

Fortunately, there are now a number of references available to help you establish retentions. A very good overall treatment of the legal issues involved in records retention is Donald Skupsky's *Recordkeeping Requirements*. This book also includes most of the more common legal requirements. (See the Bibliography at the end of this book for information on all of the publications mentioned here.)

Skupsky also offers an annually updated four-volume loose-leaf publication that contains all federal and state requirements related to records retention. Another source is the *Guide to Record Retention Requirements*, published annually by the Office of the Federal Register. This publication summarizes key federal requirements and is available at a nominal cost.

If your company is heavily regulated by a particular agency, it's a good idea to obtain the appropriate Title(s) of the federal regulations pertaining to your industry and review the retention requirements listed in it. For example, a pharmaceutical company would be interested in Title 21, Food and Drugs, while a stock brokerage firm would be concerned with Title 17, Commodity and Securities Exchange. (The various federal regulations, as well as the *Guide to Record Retention Requirements* are available from the U.S. Government Printing Office.)

The Role of Legal Counsel in the Retention Process

Your next question probably is "Can't I turn all this over to our corporate legal staff and let them figure it out?" Possibly, but don't count on it. While some attorneys are quite knowledgeable on records retention, many are not. If you simply hand your legal staff a list of records and say "How long should we keep these?" you may wait a very long time for an answer.

A better approach I've found is to do some of the homework yourself. Start with the administrative values requested by your department heads. Then use the legal resources mentioned previously to review the retentions and modify them as needed to comply with legal requirements. Record the appropriate legal citation on the inventory form where it says "legal retention."

Your legal staff can then review the proposed retentions and modify them as they feel is appropriate. This approach expedites matters considerably. However, while you can do the "legwork," it is imperative that legal counsel approve the schedule. If you do not have in-house legal staff, then hire your company's outside legal counsel to review the schedule. If the schedule ever becomes a factor in litigation, whether or not the schedule had legal approval is one of the first issues that will be raised.

Legal input is important for another reason. Your attorneys know what types of litigation your organization is likely to be involved in and which records typically need to be produced. Records are a double-edged sword. Sometimes having a record can aid your cause; sometimes it can harm it. For example, employee medical records can prove that the company tested an employee in compliance with the law and the test revealed no medical problems. Hence, keeping these records even longer than the Occupational Safety and Health Administration's requirement of thirty years after termination might be beneficial.

On the other hand, a memo questioning quality control on a product could be detrimental to the company. In fact, as a general rule, you're better off setting short retention periods (such as current year plus one prior year) for general collections of letters and memos. These items are costly to review in case of litigation and more often than not are harmful to a company's case.

Keep in mind, too, that in spite of the large number of retention requirements, many record categories are not addressed by law. For these records, the organization's administrative needs should suffice as the retention. Another rough rule of thumb, if you're really unsure as to the retention and no legal statute exists, is to set a three year retention. In fact, some states mandate a three year retention for any business records not specifically addressed in a statute.

Statutory Requirements vs. Statutes of Limitation

As you review the legal requirements, note the difference between statutory requirements and statutes of limitation. A statutory requirement is a law requiring an organization to keep a record for a certain period of time. A statute of limitation is not a requirement to keep the records but a statement that the organization is legally accountable for an action for a certain period of time.

For example, contracts are governed by state laws on statutes of limitation. That is, the company may be sued concerning that contract for so many years after the contract's expiration. Depending on the state and the type of contract, the statute of limitations might be anything from two to fifteen years. In these situations, risk assessment enters the retention process. I have had general counsel want retentions of four, six, and ten years after contract expiration. While the statute of limitations might be longer, their assessment is that the risk of a legal problem arising after so many years is minimal. In situations such as this, legal advice is critical.

Legal Issues With Electronic Information

As discussed earlier, all records are not on paper. One area to pay special attention to is "electronic mail" (E-mail), or the practice of sending messages via computer from one individual to another. While E-mail can eliminate a great deal of "telephone tag," it also can create some problems. Depending on how your computer system is backed up, messages may be captured on a system backup and retained for a long period of time.

Imagine this scenario. You're out of town, and someone sends you a request to do something that is clearly against company policy. When you return, you refuse the request. The request might have been captured on a monthly system backup, but the response might have been verbal or might have been erased after receipt. A records search required by litigation that just revealed the request and not the response could be quite damaging.

Also, people tend to communicate informally by E-mail, much as they talk on the telephone. One company's search of E-mail messages that had been captured on backups revealed not only items like the preceding example that could be misinterpreted, but also both frivolous and X-rated communications. While these might not cost the company a court case, they certainly don't enhance the firm's image. And E-mail communications have figured in many court cases. Attorneys are well aware of the legal ramifications of E-mail and regularly request electronic records during the discovery aspect of litigation.

What's the answer? It's not to discontinue E-mail, but to add some safeguards to the system. Many firms have adopted a multifaceted approach. First, backups for E-mail systems are performed separately and kept for a very brief period such as three months.

While this may involve some changes in backup procedures, it's usually worth the effort. Second, these firms educate users through training sessions and written communications. Basically, they explain that electronic mail is not the same as a phone conversation and that professional judgment should be used when sending a message, just as when you write a letter.

Finally, when users are added to the computer network, they sign a statement that they will use the computer only for business purposes, that they understand they are creating corporate records when they enter information, and that they will use the computer in a professional manner. While this does not guarantee that employees will act responsibly, it does give the organization the right to take action if the computer is misused.

And, of course, E-mail is not the only electronic record on the system. Destroying a paper copy of a memo, for example, is pointless if the same document remains on the computer. As discussed in Chapter 5, critical computer files should be inventoried and retentions assigned to them. The best approach I've found for dealing with the remaining mass of memos, letters, and such on users' systems is to establish a policy similar to the one shown in Exhibit 6-1.

Fiscal/Tax Value

In a typical organization, approximately one half of the records are financial in nature and many of these have tax implications. Those records should be retained for a minimum of the Internal Revenue Service (IRS) statutes of limitation (generally speaking, three years from the date the return is filed or due, whichever is later). However, some state statutes of limitation for tax records exceed the IRS requirements. If your company is taxed in one of these states, your retentions will need to comply with the state requirements.

Moreover, the IRS has specific retention requirements for records on computer-readable media (IRS Revenue Procedure 91-59) that must be complied with. In general, electronic tax-related accounting records must be kept *in a retrievable form* for the same period of time as the supporting hard copy. Thus, when the accounting computer system is upgraded, the company must retain the ability to read the old computer files. This may mean a costly

Exhibit 6-1. Sample Electronic Records Retention Policy

Since files on Knightly, Inc., computers are corporate records, individuals creating records on such computers are responsible for maintaining and disposing of these records in accordance with corporate policy. Users should also be aware that because these files are corporate records, they may be required for litigation or subpoenaed. Files maintained on a computer should be created with the same professionalism as hard-copy documentation.

All computer files should be maintained in accordance with the electronic-file retention guidelines listed below. However, it's a good practice to review the files on your system every three months and delete those files for which you have no further use. Unnecessary files consume disk space, may slow down your system's operation, and could have to be produced in response to litigation.

The following retention guidelines apply to electronic files: All user created files that have not been accessed or updated within one year should be deleted. This requirement applies to files on diskette, as well as to files on hard drives or the network.

The only exceptions to this one year retention period are electronic records listed on the corporate retention schedule with specific retention periods, and templates. A template is a user file that is a pattern, guide, or format used as a standard for producing data or information but that contains no personalized information. Examples include form letters, standard paragraphs, and spreadsheet formats. Templates may be retained for as long as they are useful.

conversion of old data to the new system. (Note: Since legal and tax requirements do change periodically, you should always verify them either through the appropriate agency or through a current reference source.)

Also, if your organization is audited annually by the IRS (virtually all large companies and some smaller ones are) and/or by the state, your tax staff has agreements with these tax agencies as to how long certain records must be retained. These agreements usually specify retention until the audit for a particular year is resolved. Hence, your first step here should be to meet with your finance/tax staff and determine what, if any, agreements exist. In many cases, the retention for tax related documents may have to be set as ATA (after tax audit), instead of a specific number of years.

Archival or Historical Value

Records can also have historical or archival value. You may remember the republishing of an early Sears, Roebuck catalog. Although the information in that catalog no longer had legal, fiscal, or administrative value, it was definitely of historical interest. For this same reason, firms often keep copies of company publications, annual reports, selected advertisements, photographs of major corporate events, and the like, permanently. Some firms have a corporate archivist who assumes the responsibility for maintaining these records. If there is no archivist, the records manager usually assumes the responsibility.

One caution, though, for any record with a permanent retention: The medium that the record is stored on may have a limited life. Over time paper will become brittle and likely to crumble, unless you have used acid-free paper that lasts for hundreds of years. Properly filmed, processed, and stored microfilm will also last for hundreds of years. With computer-readable media, the issue is not so much the life of the media as the ability to obtain the hardware necessary to access the data. I am old enough to remember 8-inch diskettes; of course, it's been many years since equipment was made to access them. Before long, drives for 5 ¼-inch diskettes will undoubtedly also be unavailable.

Setting the Final Retention Value

Normally, the retention period on the schedule will be the longest of the four values. And, of course, many records may only have one or two retention values, such as administrative or administrative and legal.

Preparing the Retention Schedule

The next step is a relatively simple one—packaging all of the information together in a retention schedule with supporting procedures and other material. If the inventory information and the final retention values have already been input into a computer data base, generating the schedule is simply a matter of formatting and running a report.

Virtually any standard relational database software can be used for the retention schedule. Or if you are using a commercial records management software package (see Chapter 7), almost all of these have a separate module for the retention schedule.

I usually include more fields in the database than I actually print out in the schedule. The additional information is of value to the records management staff, although a user of the schedule does not need it to determine if a record should be kept.

Typical database fields are:

- Department name
- Department number
- Record control code (optional—a unique identifier assigned to each record series, such as FIN 03–01)
- Record title
- Form or report number
- Description of the record
- Whether or not the record is vital (this is discussed in Chapter 9)
- Medium the record is kept on
- Office retention
- Retention in storage
- Legal citation for retention, if any
- Comments (a field for any notes you might have such as "consider reducing retention to six years when schedule is revised")

Exhibit 6-2 is a sample of an entry in a retention database, while Exhibit 6-3 is a sample of a portion of a retention schedule. Usually I sort the retention schedule first by department number, then alphabetically by record title. Sorting by department number tends to be most helpful as a department can quickly identify what records it is responsible for and how long it should keep them.

The schedule and the supporting materials should all be part of the records manual. Chapter 13 discusses the entire manual, but it's appropriate to consider here what material is needed to explain and support the retention schedule.

You'll need a discussion on "how to use the retention schedule." Here you'll state how the records are organized on the sched-

Exhibit 6-2. Retention Database Sample

Dept. No.:	345
Dept. Name:	Accounts Payable
Record Control Code:	FIN 03-01
Record Title:	Invoices--Vendor--Paid
Description:	Invoice, purchase order, purchase requisition, receiving report, and check copy. Filed by vendor number.
Vital:	No
Media:	Paper
Office:	1 yr.
Storage:	ATA *(after tax audit)*
Legal Cit.:	IRS
Comments:	Currently occupies 15 four-drawer lateral cabinets; evaluate for conversion to electronic document imaging

ule (i.e., by department, then title) and explain any codes or abbreviations used. For example, while most retentions can be given in years, some will be event driven. Codes to reflect these retentions might include:

AC   After completion, expiration, or settlement, as with projects, contracts, agreements, etc. Thus 1AC is one year after completion.

AD   After disposal, as with property and equipment

AT   After termination (employees, for example)

ATA   After tax audit
P   Permanent (use this one sparingly!)

Exhibit 6-3. Retention Schedule Sample

Dept. No.	Record Title	Rpt. No.	Medium	Office	Storage
803	Employee attendance report	HR29	PA	3	0
803	Employee handbook		PA	P	0
803	Employment applications— not hired		PA	1	0
803	I-9 immigration forms		PA	AT	3
803	Performance appraisals		PA	3	0
803	Personnel files		PA	AT	6

Some records managers prefer to avoid abbreviations and spell out all phrases. While this approach uses more space, it makes the schedule a little more user friendly.

You should also include a discussion of duplicate records and retention practices for general categories of records that are maintained by a number of different departments. Exhibit 6-4 is an example of a portion of such a discussion.

Getting the Schedule Approved

The next step in the process is the most critical of all—getting approval for the schedule. Here, if you're not careful, the whole process can come to a screeching halt. I've known schedules to languish on top management desks for over a year waiting for approval. Before we discuss how to avoid that pitfall, let's consider who should approve the schedule.

Obviously, organizational practice for getting policies and procedures approved varies from company to company. However, as a general rule, I've found that the following sequence works well.

The first step is to send each department head his or her respective schedule for review. Because you don't want to follow up

Exhibit 6-4. General Record Categories—Duplicate Records

Certain categories of records have duplicates retained by a number of departments. This list identifies the department responsible for holding the "official" copy or the "copy of record." The record is also listed on that department's retention schedule. This list also gives the maximum time period that another department may hold a duplicate of the record. However, the duplicates are not listed on the retention schedule under each department that might have them.

This list also specifies the retention policy for general categories of records that are originated by a number of different departments, such as various correspondence files.

Correspondence and Memos

Keep chronological correspondence files for the current year plus one prior year. The same retention applies to other collections of general or miscellaneous correspondence. Correspondence relating to a particular subject should be filed with that topic and retained for the same period of time. The same guidelines apply to internal memoranda.

Financial Records

The accounting department keeps the official copy of the following records:

Budget reports
Check requests
Employee expense reports
Invoices
Time cards

Other departments should keep these records for no longer than one year.

---

on all of these people individually, the cover memo should state that they have two weeks (or whatever time seems appropriate) to review the material. If you don't hear from them by then, you will assume they are comfortable with the schedule and send it on to legal, tax, and senior management.

The next step is the legal and tax review. Members of senior management are unlikely to approve the schedule unless they know that the legal and tax departments have approved it, as well as their own department heads.

After you receive the blessing of the legal and tax staff, then the schedule should go to senior management. Here corporate practices vary. Some organizations have each vice president approve the schedule for his or her area; others also have the CEO or even the board of directors approve the entire schedule.

Often reviewers are hesitant to approve the schedule because they feel unsure of their knowledge in this area. Several things will help speed the process.

First, be sure they understand how the schedule was prepared and who has already reviewed it. For example, the legal department needs to know what preliminary steps you have taken, using available resources, to review legal requirements for various records. It's also a good idea to print out the "legal citation" field from the database on the copy you send to legal.

Second, ask legal, tax, and service management to set their own deadlines for reviewing the material. People are more likely to meet a deadline if they set it. This practice also helps with sensitive egos, who might resent your asking them to do something by a particular date. Of course, you'll confirm the deadline in writing with a "thank-you" memo.

Third, a few days before the material is due back, give the reviewers a "friendly reminder." That's a phone call to ask if they have any questions so far—much more tactful than "Have you looked at it yet?" And if they live on Olympus and don't talk to ordinary mortals, give the reminder to their administrative assistants.

Usually these approaches work, but if they don't, calculate approximately how many records could be destroyed if the schedule is approved and what the current cost of storing those records is. This statistic usually gets everyone's attention.

It's also a good idea to place a moratorium on buying filing cabinets until the schedule is in place. Once the schedule is approved, the file cabinets probably won't be needed as so many records can be sent to storage or destroyed. Also, people will run out of space for records, and this will motivate them to expedite the schedule approval process.

Another highly effective approach is to ask for approval of the schedule at a senior staff meeting. You send out the schedule ahead of time with memos from legal and tax indicating their approval. Then at the meeting, you ask for immediate approval.

I have used this technique successfully when the schedule had to be approved promptly so records could be destroyed before a forthcoming move. At one company, we asked for approval, and the CEO said, "I reviewed it carefully over the weekend. Looks good to me. Any problems?" Not surprisingly, there were none.

Implementing the Schedule

Getting a policy approved is one thing. Getting it implemented is another. If you simply mail out the schedule with a cover letter, nothing will happen. It's not that people purposely are trying to sabotage the program, but they are busy and the schedule becomes one of those things they'll do when they have time, which is never.

A better approach is to distribute the schedule at training sessions. I usually have two types of sessions. The first is a short one for managers, emphasizing the rationale behind the program and asking for their cooperation in ensuring their areas comply. If possible, I get a representative from legal or senior management to "drop in" and say a few words about the program's importance.

The second type of session is a "nuts and bolts" one for anyone who will be actively involved in implementing the program. I try to keep the group size small—twenty or fewer is a good guideline. If the group is much larger, people don't ask questions and their minds tend to wander.

In this session, I review all of the procedures for the program: how to use the schedule, how to dispose of the records, how to box records and send them to storage, and so on. While all of these procedures are written in the manual, I've found that going over them orally substantially improves compliance.

After the training sessions comes the "file purge." Specific days are set aside for implementing the schedule—a day for reviewing the files and disposing of all records past their retention and a day for boxing up records that should go to storage. This effort should be coordinated with building services so that you have plenty of strong bodies available to haul away the trash and transport the boxes to storage.

If properly presented and promoted, this event can be a rather enjoyable break from routine activities. Many companies allow employees to dress more casually on these days; some order in pizza or provide snack food. Some of my clients give records co-ordinators a small token of appreciation for their efforts such as T-shirts or paperweights.

Keep track of how many records are disposed of and how many boxes go to storage—you'll be pleasantly surprised at the results. You may also want to take some photographs or have the event featured in the company newsletter or magazine.

Conducting Departmental Records Audits

At this point, you may feel your work is done. However, even with all of the preceding steps, some individuals may not comply with the program. Their failure to comply wastes resources and may even jeopardize the legal credibility of the program.

For these reasons, some of my clients conduct departmental records audits after the annual file purge is completed. No, this does not necessarily mean more work for you. While the records manager sets the audit standards, he or she does not necessarily perform the audit. Some organizations incorporate it into their an-nual operational audits performed by internal auditors. This ap-proach saves your time and gives added credibility to the process because most firms place great importance on internal audit findings.

If your organization does not have internal audits, typically either the records manager or an external consultant performs the audit. Some of my clients quite frankly admit they'd rather I do the audit so that their relationships with other managers are not endangered if problems are found on the audit.

Since the purpose of an audit is not to "catch" people but to ensure that standards are being met, audit standards should be communicated in advance. I also have no problem with managers knowing in advance when the audit will occur. Yes, they may scurry around to "get their act together" before the audit, but that's fine. I want them to be in compliance; I don't really care what has motivated the compliance.

While audit standards vary, depending on the scope of the records management program, typically they include:

- Verifying that the records coordinator has an up-to-date copy of the records manual.
- Checking all major record categories—regardless of media—to ensure that the department is in compliance with the retention schedule.
- Spot-checking individual offices and computer terminals to ensure that duplicate files are not kept beyond their retention and that electronic files are being purged in compliance with the policy.
- Verifying compliance with any other organizational records management criteria.

The audit report should detail all findings and indicate what follow-up actions should occur.

Audits do work. I've noticed dramatic compliance improvements in those clients I audit annually. Many departmental coordinators tell me that the threat of the audit is what motivates the managers in their departments to dispose of records properly. Most coordinators are administrative assistants or secretaries; hence, they do not have the authority to make a manager comply with the policy. The audit provides the support they need.

Updating the Schedule

Records retention is not a one-time activity; it's an ongoing process. The first step in that process is an annual updating of the schedule. When a schedule is never revised, people begin to distrust it. They suspect, quite rightly, that the standards set five or ten years ago are no longer appropriate, and they start disregarding the schedule.

Each year the records coordinators should review the entries for their departments with all appropriate personnel within the department. Record categories that are no longer maintained should be dropped from the schedule, and new categories should be added as necessary. Retentions for existing records should be reviewed to see if they are still appropriate.

The records manager should check current legal sources to see if any legal requirements have been added or changed. All changes to the schedule should be reviewed and approved by appropriate management personnel including legal and tax.

After the schedule is revised, it's a good idea to have training sessions for any new personnel who may have joined the company since the last series of sessions.

The next step in the process is the file purge. Making this an annual event does a great deal to ensure compliance with the program. Scheduling it approximately two to four months after year-end usually works well. Holding it immediately after the year-end means records created near the end of the year may still be active. If they're sent to storage, they often need to be retrieved almost immediately. Waiting a few months eliminates this problem.

Of course, departments don't have to wait for file purge days to send inactive records to storage or destroy records past their retention. But you'll find overall compliance with the retention schedule is much higher if you have days set aside to devote to "housecleaning" the files.

After the file purge comes the departmental records audit. When the audit and any necessary follow-ups are complete, take a few minutes to congratulate yourself on a job well done. And remember, it gets easier each year as employees get more comfortable with the records management concept.

Modifying the Schedule: Acquisitions

Even the best records management programs can go into a tailspin when confronted with an acquisition. When your company acquires another company, it often ends up with that company's records as well. I've known records managers suddenly to find out they now have 20,000 more boxes of inactive records than they had the day before. We'll talk about coping with the boxes in Chapter 7, but let's address modifying the retention schedule now.

The acquired company may have a retention schedule, but

don't count on it. And even if it does, the schedule is probably inconsistent with yours in some key areas. You have two alternatives. The first is to convert the company to your schedule, adding new categories as necessary. The second is to develop a separate schedule for the company, but one that is consistent with yours. This approach is usually done when the acquired company is remaining a separate entity at its own place of business with its own staff. Whichever approach you choose, you should address the situation as quickly as possible.

Typical Results

Implementing a comprehensive records retention program will "free up" significant amounts of office space. Consider the following statistics from an ARMA (Association of Records Managers and Administrators) survey of companies implementing a records retention program for the first time. On an average, 24.1 percent of the total volume of a company's records are destroyed when a retention program is begun. Another 32.3 percent of the records are sent to inactive storage in a records center. And only 43.6 percent of the records remain in the office area. In other words, over half the office space occupied by records is now available for other uses.

7

The Records Center
Part I: Storage Options and Indexing Records in Storage

In records management, the term "records center" is used to indicate a central storage area for the company's inactive records—those records that must be kept but are not used frequently enough to justify high-cost office storage.

The increasing use of computer-readable media has not and will not eliminate the need for records centers, although it may eventually reduce the volume of paper stored off-site. In spite of, or perhaps because of, computers, paper sales increase every year. And, if records are going to be kept for only a few years, it is cheaper to store them on paper than to convert them to microfilm or optical disk.

Records Center Options

Because they are designed for inactive records, records centers should provide economical storage while permitting relatively prompt retrieval. Meeting these dual objectives means choosing from among three basic alternatives for storing inactive records:

1. An on-site records center
2. An off-site facility operated by the company
3. A commercial records center

Let's examine the pros and cons of each option.

On-Site Records Centers

Storing inactive records on-site is a common practice for companies (often small- to medium-size) that have available space within their buildings. Usually these companies own their buildings and are located in areas with comparatively inexpensive real estate. While it would hardly be economical to rent office space in midtown Manhattan to store inactive records, if the company owns a building in Dubuque, Iowa, with space to spare, an on-site center might be its best option.

Usually on-site centers are located in the basement or on the ground floor, so that the weight of the records does not strain the building unduly. Also, transferring records in and out of the building is simplified because elevators are not involved. Basements, however, can be vulnerable to flooding.

An on-site records center should have adequate fire protection, security, and lighting, as well as all the other physical characteristics of records centers that are discussed later in this chapter. The on-site center is *not* a large storeroom for departmental Christmas decorations or other infrequently used items. The center should be used only for records.

Off-Site Company-Operated Records Centers

Large organizations sometimes build or lease totally separate records center buildings. This approach is viable when the company has a very large amount of inactive records. Other organizations segregate a portion of an existing warehouse and establish an off-site records center there. This approach is feasible if the company already has one or more warehouses (possibly used to store products).

Such space is usually less expensive than space in the company's office buildings, yet it allows the company to maintain direct control of its own records. Of course, key considerations here are the security and accessibility of the warehouse.

The Commercial Records Center

The third alternative is using a commercial records center. These facilities are designed exclusively for records storage and provide a wide range of services, including the retrieval and destruction of records at your request.

If the company does not have available storage space, using a commercial facility may be the only option. Some companies with available space still opt to use a commercial facility because they don't want to incur the capital expenditures needed for an in-house facility or to maintain the staff necessary to support it. As more businesses "outsource" support services, the popularity of commercial records centers has increased.

There's no easy rule as to whether an in-house operation is cheaper or not. If the company does have low cost storage space, the in-house operation is usually cheaper in the long run. However, the "long run" may be a payback of five, seven, or nine years, and many companies require a quicker return on capital investments.

Of course, financial considerations are not the only ones. Some companies opt for in-house facilities because they don't want company records to leave company premises. A company in a rural location simply may not have access to a reliable commercial vendor. Others organizations opt for commercial centers because they require less effort and internal resources than managing an in-house facility. Most organizations use commercial centers for computer-readable media and microfilm because these items require a climate controlled facility with constant temperature and humidity.

If you decide to use a commercial facility, the decision should be made carefully. There are many very reputable, highly professional facilities, but there are also some less than desirable operations.

Services

The first step is determining what services you need and making sure the suppliers under consideration can provide them.

Media to be stored. Some centers store only paper records and others only microfilm and computer-readable media, but most store all types of media. Typically they have special climate-controlled vaults for film and magnetic media and use regular warehouse space for paper.

Computer indexing of your records. A steadily increasing number of commercial centers provide computerized indexing services. This is a highly desirable feature and well worth the cost. As part of such a system, the center should be able to provide you with a monthly printout listing which cartons are due for destruction (based on retention data you supply). The center should also be able to generate index listings by department so each department can have a printout of its holdings. Likewise, the center should be able to break down your monthly invoice by department so you can internally charge each department back for the storage costs it incurs.

Some centers' systems are sophisticated enough for you to access your records index by a modem. While you cannot change any of the data in the system, you can view your holdings at any time. This eliminates the need for monthly printouts and also lets you verify when data has been entered into the system.

A couple of cautions here: Be sure you and the center agree in advance, in writing, as to exactly what level of indexing will be done. Also reach agreement as to how much time will elapse between when the records are received and when the index information is entered into the computer.

Specify that the indexing must be accurate, and check to make sure that it is. In one case, I found errors in data entry for 50 percent of the boxes. The project was a large conversion, and the supplier was using untrained temporaries to input the data.

Finally, make sure the center backs up the index regularly and stores the backup in another location. Yes, this sounds incredibly obvious, but I know of a case where the center did not back up the index, "lost" the entire database, and had to recreate it manually, which took months!

Pick-up service. Most centers provide pick-up and delivery service for a fee. Usually, records are picked up the next day, but find out in advance what the center's practice is and when delays might occur.

Retrieval of records. You usually have several choices in terms of retrieval. Normal service is delivering the requested record the following day, although some firms provide same-day service if the request is received early in the morning. "Rush" delivery (usually within two hours) is available at a substantially higher cost. An increasing number of centers will fax the record to you—an attractive alternative (if you only need a few pages) as you get the record quickly for comparatively little cost.

One issue you'll need to address is whether you want the center to pull a specific file or pages from a file out of the box or to send you the entire box. Most centers will do it either way, but some only deliver entire boxes. Of course, the files in the boxes will need to be in good order if the center staff are to pull specific records.

Also find out the procedure and charges for requesting a record after normal working hours or during a weekend. This is especially important if you're storing computer media or if your organization is a twenty-four-hours-a-day business such as a hospital.

On-site client work area. At times, someone from your company may need to "browse" through a number of boxes of records, possibly as part of an audit or in response to litigation. In these circumstances, it's much easier to send one or more staff people to the records center than to send hundreds of boxes to your office. Many commercial centers have an audit room available for clients to use for such searches.

Destruction of records. Most facilities will handle the destruction of records past their retention upon receipt of a written authorization from a designated individual at your company. If desired, they will shred the records and certify the confidentiality of the destruction, with an extra charge for this service.

Other Considerations

Of course, level of service is not the only consideration in selecting a commercial records storage facility. There are several other issues.

The physical facility. Be sure to visit any facility you are seriously considering. The pictures in the brochure sometimes bear little relation to reality. While records centers are not glamorous, the facility should be neat and orderly. The building itself should be fire resistant. The paper records storage area should be sprinklered, while the storage area for microfilm and magnetic media should have a chemical fire extinguishing system. The facility should have both fire and security alarms with direct tie-ins to the fire department and police department.

Yes, I did say sprinklered. The water damage from sprinklers going off (and they only go off where the fire is) is far less than the damage from either an uncontrolled fire or the fire department's hoses. The National Fire Protection Association (NFPA) has a standard for the protection of records (ANSI/NFPA 232) and a manual for fire protection for archives and records centers (ANSI/NFPA 232AM; see the Bibliography). NFPA 232AM specifically addresses fire protection in large records storage facilities, and any center you consider should be in compliance with it.

Staffing. Find out whom you will be dealing with on a regular basis (usually not the person who sells you the service). Do you feel comfortable with their level of expertise and attitude? How available are they? Who is the backup in their absence? Also find out if security checks are made on all personnel working at the center and if employees are bonded.

References. In addition to checking the references provided by the center, which, of course, will be positive, use your ARMA (Association of Records Managers and Administrators) contacts. Ask other records managers in the area whom they use and their level of satisfaction.

Also find out if the company is a member of the Association of Commercial Records Centers—the professional group for these businesses. While belonging is not an absolute guarantee of quality, members are required to subscribe to a code of ethics and most reputable companies are members. The association can provide you with the names of members in your area. (See the Appendix for the association's address.)

Cost. Comparing prices on records centers is always a bit of a challenge. You pay a separate charge for each activity they perform: shelving, indexing, storage, retrieval, destruction, and so on. And you'll find one center will be lower on one item and higher on another. What I do is quantify what a firm's annual usage is likely to be (i.e., how many boxes going in, going out, being stored, retrieved, etc.) and cost out each center under that scenario.

There are two charges meriting special attention. The first is cartons. Does the center require you to use their cartons and, if so, are they competitively priced? Some centers charge considerably more for the cartons than you would pay if you bought them directly from a carton vendor. While I don't believe a center should require you to use its cartons, it is fair for it to require you to use cartons of a certain quality and size. If you send over records in old copier paper cartons and the bottoms fall out when their people pick up the boxes, they'll understandably be aggrieved. And since the shelving is designed to handle boxes of a particular size, odd-sized boxes don't use space efficiently and may not fit on the shelves.

The second charge to watch for is the cost of permanently removing your records. Some centers have a very high charge for permanent removal (usually approximately one year's storage for a box). This charge is designed to make it difficult for you to cost justify removing your records, even though you are unhappy with their service. I always try to have this charge removed from the contract. You should not be financially penalized for a supplier's poor service. However, in some regions, all suppliers have the charge, and it is virtually impossible to get it eliminated from the contract.

If you're already using a center with a high permanent removal fee and are dissatisfied, don't despair. Often another center will agree to pay the removal fee if you decide to move your records to their facility.

Company Records Centers

If you do your "homework," you normally can find a quality commercial operation that will meet your needs well. But if you decide that a company-operated facility, whether on- or off-site, is best for your organization, you'll find the following information helpful. (Also see Chapter 8.)

Design

Both company-operated and commercial records centers tend to be remarkably similar in physical design. Moreover, the design guidelines have changed relatively little in the past thirty years for a simple reason—no one has found a better way.

Off-site company records centers generally are single-level concrete structures with windows limited to office and entry areas. Such a structure provides good security and fire protection. The building's ceiling is generally at least 15 feet high to allow maximum use of space through shelving tiers and stacked cartons. Obviously, an on-site center will probably have lower ceilings and the storage area may not be windowless.

In addition to an area for records storage, the center should have adequate office space for its staff and a work area for center users. Just as in a commercial center, individuals may need to browse through several cartons. Having a work area means the cartons don't have to leave the center and allows users to request other cartons easily.

When microfilm, magnetic media, videotapes, or audio tapes are stored in the center, temperature and humidity should be strictly controlled. Otherwise, if the climate permits, a good ventilation and heating system may suffice. In any case, the office and work area should be air conditioned for the comfort of their users.

As we've already discussed, good fire protection is essential. The center should comply with the NFPA standards discussed earlier. No smoking should be allowed in the records storage areas. And while for security reasons there may be only one entrance to the records center, there should be other fire exits. Emergency procedures should be reviewed carefully with all center employees, and fire drills conducted regularly.

Although fire is the most obvious danger, records centers do have the potential for a variety of accidents. Pulpit-type ladders (i.e., ladders with a platform to hold cartons) should be used to avoid accidents when shelving or removing cartons. All staff should be trained in proper lifting procedures to avoid back injuries, and job descriptions should specify what weight the individuals should be able to lift regularly (usually 40 or 50 pounds). This latter requirement is not sex discrimination; it's bad-back, slipped-disk discrimination. And, since the passage of ADA (The Americans with Disabilities Act), it is especially important that job descriptions address thoroughly any physical requirements of the position.

Be sure that all shelving is properly installed by a reliable contractor. In at least one records center, the collapse of poorly installed shelving resulted in a death. If your company has a safety manager or OSHA (Occupational Safety and Health Administration) expert, have this individual inspect the center and make any appropriate recommendations.

The records center should have both phone and facsimile service. Facsimile is especially helpful if the records center is off-site. Good lighting is also important. While this may sound obvious, be sure the shelving is not installed directly under the light fixtures, thus blocking the light. Again, this has happened more than once. If possible, the lighting system should be wired so that the lights in each aisle and/or section can be turned on and off separately to conserve energy.

Cartons and Shelving

For the actual storage of paper records, a combination of standard size cartons and steel shelving will keep costs down, use space efficiently, and permit quick retrieval. For these reasons, most records centers use a system similar or identical to the one outlined as follows.

The standard storage container is made of double-wall, 200-pound corrugated cardboard with handholds for ease in carrying. The carton is 15 inches long, 12 inches wide, and 10 inches high. This versatile container can hold legal-size files along the 15-inch length and letter-size files along the 12-inch width. When removed from their binders, computer printouts will lie flat in the carton. These containers are assembled easily and can be stored flat when not in use to reduce storage space.

I would avoid the longer 24- and 30-inch boxes. They do not hold up as well because they are so heavy when fully loaded. The weight also makes them unwieldy for office staff to load and handle. Indexing records is more of a problem, too. Because of their greater capacity, you're more likely to end up with several different types of records in a box, which complicates indexing, retrieval, and destruction of the records.

You have a choice as to lids. My preference is for the "shoe box" style lift off lid as it makes searching for records in the box easier. However, some records managers prefer single unit boxes with a foldover lid. They feel this eliminates lost lids. (Personally, I think lids procreate! It seems like every time a major reboxing is completed a surplus of lids results.)

I recommend that you avoid the combination corrugated and steel pull-out file units that are stacked on top of each other. Some users experience difficulty in opening drawers near the bottom of the stack and find that the units do not wear well. Also these units are costly, difficult to transport, and require more aisle space than cartons stacked on shelving.

The shelving itself may be steel, particle board, or plywood, while the uprights are, of course, steel. Steel shelving is the most durable, but also the most costly. The shelving units are usually 42 inches wide and 30 inches deep, with 23 inches between shelves. Each shelf holds twelve cartons (three across, two deep, and two high). To conserve space further, two shelving units may be fastened together along the 42-inch width. Thus, to get to an inner box, a maximum of three boxes would be moved.

Usually the aisles between the rows of shelves are 30 to 36 inches wide. The main "feeder" aisles are 4 to 6 feet wide, depending on the type of equipment (forklift truck, hand cart, etc.) that must pass down them.

Organizing the Records

To use available space most effectively, don't segregate records in the center by department. Instead place the cartons in any available space and assign box numbers to denote the locations. (Of course, you wouldn't mix more than one department's records within a box.) To retrieve a particular carton, the center staff simply checks the index to determine the box number and then locates the record accordingly.

While you are not grouping boxes by department, there are some practical considerations in shelving cartons to keep in mind. Some box locations are less accessible than others. For example, if you butt shelving units together, the boxes in the inner core will be less accessible. Also, boxes on the bottom shelf and on the very highest shelves are harder to access. You may want to shelve boxes with low retrieval needs and long retentions in these areas.

Assigning Box Numbers

You'll also need a numbering system to ensure speedy retrieval of the boxes. The best practice is to assign two numbers to each box. The first number is the location number. You might consider this the box's "street address," as this number tells you where to find the box. I normally use a three part numbering system. The first number identifies the row the box is on, the second number the shelving unit, and the third number the box's location on that shelving unit. For example, 5-3-36 would mean row 5, shelving unit 3, box 36. Since there are twelve boxes to a shelf, box 36 would be on the third shelf up from the bottom. Or you might prefer to identify the rows by letters of the alphabet, making the box E-3-36. Shelving rows and units should have signs or labels indicating their number or letter.

Bar coding cartons and shelves is an alternative to using location numbers. Each box is bar coded. (The control number can serve as the bar code reference.) The shelves are also bar coded at regular intervals. When a box is shelved, both its bar code and the shelf's bar code are scanned, thus entering the box's location into the computer. With this system, boxes do not have to be returned to their original location. Instead, returned boxes can be shelved anywhere because the new location is scanned at the time of reshelving. This system allows more effective space utilization and faster checkouts.

Since location numbers will be reused if a box is destroyed, it's a good practice to assign each box a control number. This number might be considered the box's Social Security number as it will not be reused. It may either be computer generated or printed in advance on the records transfer forms (much as check numbers are printed on checks). The number can be consecutively issued (000001, 000002, etc.) or it might be based on the year (95–0001, 95–0002, etc.).

Indexing the Records

An index is essential for the successful operation of any records center. Users should not have to supply box numbers when they request a record, and you should know from the index exactly what boxes you have in the center and where they are located.

Computerizing the Index

Regardless of the size of your records center, I strongly advocate computerizing the index. An automated index will speed retrieval, reduce records center staff labor, and improve your control over the records in the center. Also, the sooner you automate, the easier the process will be. Having worked with conversions of different size facilities, I can assure you it's much easier to convert 3,000 boxes to an automated system than 43,000.

Once the decision is made to computerize the index, a whole string of other decisions must follow. One of the first is the level of detail the index should address. Do you want to index every document in a box, every file in a box, or just the overall contents of the box? Most organizations primarily index the overall contents of the box, as the amount of data entry involved in indexing every file or document is significant. If the records are in the box in a specific order, finding a particular file is not difficult. For example, if the 1994 paid invoices are boxed in vendor number order and the box's contents are vendors 19381 to 19492, it's easy to locate 19451.

Of course, there may be some instances where it is desirable to index each file or document separately. A hospital sending inactive patient files to storage might want to index each file by patient number. Most computerized systems can be designed to accommodate both approaches.

Another set of decisions involves hardware and software. The number of boxes in storage and the amount of information you want to capture on each will affect the amount of computer memory you need. The number of individuals needing to access the system and the level of sophistication of your organization's computer system will determine whether you use a stand-alone computer or a networked system. Your best approach is to discuss your needs with the systems department and see what approach they recommend and how long it will take to implement it.

The first step in a software decision is choosing between a commercial package and an internally developed system. There are a wide range of commercial packages on the market now. Many of the packages have been available for several years. Most are designed to run on a personal computer and can be networked, although a few packages are designed solely for a large computer system.

Several considerations should affect your decision:

▪ Can the commercial package meet all your needs? Before evaluating packages, identify what you want the system to do. Then see how well each package meets that list of objectives.

▪ What is the supplier's history like? Evaluate its track record carefully. How long has the company been in business? How many systems have they installed? What kind of training and support will they provide your staff? How heavily dependent on their support will you be?

▪ How does the cost, level of support, and quality compare with an internally developed system? This is the ultimate question, and I've found the answer varies from organization to organization. Prices on commercial records management packages are coming down, and access to in-house programming staff is difficult at some organizations. On the other hand, I've also seen in-house staff develop a very satisfactory program at a fraction of the cost of a commercial package.

▪ How much material is in storage? If you're storing a couple of hundred boxes, it would be difficult to justify buying a commercial package costing a few thousand dollars. (And most commercial packages are in this price range.) With such a low volume, systems staff support also may be difficult to obtain. You'll probably find yourself setting up a rudimentary database along the lines discussed later in this chapter using whichever PC database your organization has selected as the company standard. And for a few hundred boxes or less, this approach will be quite satisfactory.

An excellent source of information on available records management software is the *Software Directory for Automated Records*

Management Systems published by the Association of Records Managers and Administrators (see the Bibliography). The directory is updated regularly and provides detailed information on a wide range of packages.

System Specifications

To choose the best software option, you need to identify exactly what you want the system to do. A records center indexing system is basically a moderately sophisticated relational database.

If you are developing the system internally, don't use a spreadsheet or word processing package. Neither one will meet your needs adequately. A functional system can be developed using most standard types of database software. (Microsoft's Access, Lotus's Approach, and Borland's Paradox are examples of generic PC database software.) If you elect this approach, select the database software with which you and your systems staff are most comfortable.

The primary database for the system will create a record for each box in storage. Typical fields would be:

Department name

Department number

Record title—or record control code, if you've assigned a standardized code to each record series, such as HR 01–01 for employee personnel files.

Date from

Date to—two date fields are preferable, rather than one with just the year as some records will be in chronological sequence.

Sequence from

Sequence to—these fields are useful when you just need to give a summary of the contents—purchase orders 07895 to 08963, for example.

Contents listing—this permits a more detailed listing of contents.

Destruction date—if your retention schedule database is linked to the index database, the system should have the ability to calculate destruction dates for you.

Date record received at records center

Contact name—whom to call if there's a question—this is especially helpful in large organizations.

Control box number—either computer generated or entered
from the records transfer form.

Locational box number

Comments—useful if you need to annotate the entry—for example, "box held for litigation; do not destroy."

Date destroyed

Destruction certified by

Whether you select a commercial package or develop a system
internally, several features are desirable. First, the records management staff should handle all data entry and be able to run both
routine and ad hoc reports without assistance. If you decide to let
other departments access the database on the network, they should
be able to view their own holdings only, not those of other departments, and they should not be able to change any information in
the system.

You also want the capability to make global changes to database fields. For example, if department number 289 is changed to
293, you don't want to have to manually change each entry. It also
should be easy to copy repetitive information from record to record. Thus, if there are 350 boxes of 1994 invoices to enter, you don't
want to have to key in "Supplier invoices" and the date 350 times.

Consider both the frequent and infrequent user of the system.
Menu-driven systems with lots of user aids are very helpful for
someone who references the database infrequently. On the other
hand, the person who is doing all the data entry and knows the
system very thoroughly doesn't want to have to go through three
sets of menus every time he or she needs to use the system. That
person needs to be able to hit a couple of keys and reach the desired part of the system.

After a box has been destroyed, you may want to transfer its
entry to a secondary or archival database or run a printout of all
destroyed cartons. Keeping a record of what has been destroyed is
helpful in case a destroyed record is requested for litigation. Then
you have proof that the record was destroyed as part of your standard records retention policy.

Another desirable feature for the computerized index is the ability to track records that have been checked out to users. This subsystem would typically include:

Name of the individual checking out the record
Department
Telephone number
Box/file checked out
Date checked out
Date due back
Date actually returned
Comments

This subsystem should also have the ability to monitor how many times a record has been checked out. This information is very helpful in determining if retention periods should be shortened because a particular record category is not being referenced.

System Reports

One major benefit of a computerized system is the ready access you have to a great deal of information about the records in storage. While the number of reports you can generate is virtually limitless, you'll find these especially helpful:

Records due for destruction—a listing of the records due to be destroyed, sorted by department.
Box activity report—a listing of which boxes have been retrieved and how often.
Department listing—a report listing records in storage by department.
Charge-out report—a listing of boxes or files that have been checked out and not returned.
Summary report—how many boxes have been added to storage, how many destroyed, and total number of boxes now in storage. Data should be listed by department and totalled for the entire organization.
Locations available—a listing of box locations available for new records.

Exhibit 7-1. Sample Records Center Index Card

Record Title			Contents					Dept. Received From		
			Alpha. or Num.		Date					
Date Received	Received By	Box Number	From	To	From	To	Date To Be Destroyed	Date Destroyed	Certified By

Manual Indexing Systems

While I don't recommend manual systems, a manual system is better than no system at all and, in some cases, due to no access to a computer or very limited resources, may be the only alternative in the short run.

There are two basic ways to set up a manual system. The first uses an index card similar to the one in Exhibit 7-1. A separate card is established for each record title in storage. When new boxes are received, they are entered on the card. While this system does not provide as much information as its automated counterpart, it is a simple way to locate records.

With the index card system, you'll also need a destruction log. When records are added to the index card, their box numbers are entered in the log under the appropriate month and year for destruction, such as January 1998. Each month, the log is checked and the appropriate departments notified of the pending destructions. When the records are destroyed, that information is recorded on the index card.

An alternative manual system uses a multipart records transfer form (one form per box). One copy of the form is filed under the department responsible for the records, and another copy is filed under the destruction date. This system eliminates the index cards and destruction log. However, you do have the risk of misfiled or misplaced forms—a not infrequent problem.

Chapter 8 discusses records transfer forms in more detail, as well as all the other day-to-day operating procedures of the center.

8

The Records Center
Part II: Operating Procedures

In addition to a comprehensive indexing system, the records center needs simple, effective procedures for transferring records into storage, retrieving them when needed, and destroying them on schedule. Let's consider the transfer process first.

Transferring Records to the Center

The first steps in the transfer process are the responsibility of the department whose records will be stored. The department requests the required number of boxes from the records center or supply room. A standard carton (as discussed in Chapter 7) holds approximately 14 inches of letter-size files or 11 inches of legal-size, so calculating the appropriate number of boxes is a simple matter.

Department personnel then assemble the boxes and fill them. Records should be left in their manila file folders and loaded in the box just as in a file drawer. This way the tops of the folders are clearly visible, and retrieval is simplified. However, records in hanging file folders should be transferred to manila folders. Hanging folders do not fit properly in the cartons, cost too much to go into storage, and take up too much space. Records in binders should be removed from them as the binders take up too much space and can be reused. Fastening bundles of records together with rubber bands is not a good idea as the bands break after a year or so. It's better to tie bundles of small items such as receipts with string or to insert them in large envelopes.

Make sure users understand that all records in a box *must* have the same destruction date. And, if possible, all the records should belong to the same record category. One of the biggest reasons for misplaced records is that someone has a couple of inches of space left in a box and throws in an odd few files to fill it out. Those files aren't indexed and are lost forever. I usually suggest that as long as the box is at least two-thirds full, the records center accept it—a little empty space is much less of a problem than lost files. Along the same lines, discourage people from stuffing the box as full as possible. Cartons do not hold up well if they are overloaded.

After the boxes are filled, the department completes a records transfer form for each box. Exhibit 8-1 is a sample transfer form. The user keeps one copy of the form as a control, until the records center acknowledges receipt of the box. The second copy serves as a data entry form for the records center. The third copy may be either a self-adhesive label affixed to the end of the box or a non-adhesive version placed inside the box.

There are two schools of thought on labeling cartons. One prefers a descriptive label on the box's end so that it's readily apparent what's inside. The other approach is to place only the box location number and control number on the label. This improves security since an unauthorized person who has gained access to the records center cannot tell what's in a box. If you adopt this second approach, include a copy of the form inside the box. That way, if the ultimate disaster occurs and the box is not indexed or is accidentally removed from the index, you can still identify its contents.

Also, write the location and control numbers in indelible felt-tip marker on the other end of the box. I realize this is like wearing a belt and suspenders, but I've known of cases where the labels had defective adhesive and came off.

When the boxes reach the records center, the first step is making sure you have received all of them. Your staff may not be able to index the boxes that day, but if a carton is lost and you don't discover it until later, it will be much more difficult to locate. You may want the department to assign temporary numbers to each box (1 of 20, 2 of 20, etc.) to aid in the verification process. You can

Exhibit 8-1. Sample Records Transfer Form

RECORDS TRANSFER FORM

96-752

Dept. Name	Dept. No.

Record Title (as listed on the retention schedule)

Date From	Date To

Filing Sequence/Contents Description

Date Sent to Center	Destruction Date

Form Prepared By

Approval of Records Coordinator

= =

Box Location (to be completed by records center)

---

also have the department submit a transfer summary, a form listing all boxes in the shipment.

The next step is verifying that the boxes belong in storage. If the records are not listed on the retention schedule for storage, you'll need to determine if they should be added to the schedule. Occasionally there will be a record category that was overlooked in the inventory but does have a legitimate need for retention. But, in most cases, the records don't belong in the records center either because long-term retention is unnecessary or because they are duplicates of what another department stores. In these situations, notify the department that you can't accept the records and, if they are past their retention, offer to destroy them.

Also be sure that the destruction date is in compliance with the retention schedule. If the date is incorrect, contact the records coordinator for that area and explain why the date has been corrected.

After the boxes are indexed, notify the department that they have been received and shelved. If you're using a computerized indexing system, the simplest method is to send the department a printout of the index entry for each box. This practice allows the department to verify your data entry. If you have a manual system, send the department a copy of the transfer form with the box's location written on it. Although the departments will not be retrieving records themselves, their comfort level will be considerably higher if they know where the boxes are.

If you are using a commercial records center, it will usually have its own forms and procedures for transferring records. In such situations, all transfers should be coordinated through the records management department. This ensures that departments only send to the center records that do belong in storage and that retention dates are set properly.

Retrieving Records From Storage

The key to user confidence in the records center is an effective retrieval process. Users should normally be able to request a record by phone, electronic mail, facsimile, or interdepartmental mail.

A key consideration in the retrieval process is deciding whether to check out the entire box to a user or just an individual file or record. My personal preference is to check out the file or document. When you check out the entire box, files may be removed from the box and not replaced. Also if anyone else needs a record from the box, you'll have to retrieve it from the current user.

Checking out specific records is especially important when records in a box might be needed by a number of different users. For example, the paid-off mortgage files at a bank might be retrieved by several different departments. If one department has a box, other departments' access to mortgages in that box is slowed down significantly.

Of course, there are exceptions to the practice of checking out specific files. Personnel and payroll records are often delivered to the records center in cartons that are taped shut because access to the files is limited to those departments. With highly confidential records such as these, the entire box should be sent to the department unopened.

The issue of access is not just limited to personnel or payroll records. You need a policy as to who may retrieve specific types of records from the records center. While some records such as the paid-off mortgages might be available for access by several departments, in general, the department sending the records to storage should be the only department able to retrieve the cartons directly. If another department needs the record, it obtains permission from the department accountable for the records. For example, if the marketing department needs a copy of an old invoice, accounts payable authorizes the invoice's retrieval. You may also want to specify who in a department may retrieve records—the department head and a designated backup, for example.

If you're using a commercial records center, all retrievals should be cleared through the records management department. The commercial center should be given a list of three or four individuals who are authorized to request records retrieval, and all requests should go through these individuals. This approach protects both you and the records center from the possibility of records being checked out to unauthorized individuals.

Commercial centers provide you with a procedure and form to use when requesting records. If you establish an in-house records center, you'll need a form similar to the one in Exhibit 8-2. This form is basically self-explanatory, with the exception of the "remarks" space at the bottom. Here records center personnel can indicate if they had any difficulty locating the record, if the requester supplied incorrect information, or if the record could not be found.

If the charge-out system is computerized, you'll need a three-part request form. If charge outs are not computerized, the form should have four parts. The user keeps one copy as a control until the record is received. Another copy is attached to the record, thus identifying it for the user. The third copy is attached to an out card placed in the box. The out card expedites refiling and also lets you know what files are out of a box.

If the indexing system is manual, the fourth copy is filed in a tickler file under the date when the record is due back in the center. A two- or three-week "check out" period is common; I prefer two weeks because requesters are less likely to misplace records in the shorter time frame. If the record is not returned by that date, a records center staff member needs to contact the user to determine if he or she still needs the record. If the charge-out system is computerized, the follow-up can be computer generated.

This follow-up procedure is essential if the integrity of the records in the center is to be preserved. Otherwise, users often forget to return the records when they are finished with them. Eventually the records become lost or misplaced.

If you are using a manual follow-up system, save the tickler file copies for the year, filing them by record title. Then at the end of the year, you'll be able to identify which record categories were accessed during the year. As discussed earlier, this is valuable data for determining which retention periods to shorten.

From a user's standpoint, delivering records in a timely manner is a critical issue. You'll need to determine what time frame you can realistically meet and commit to it. If your records center is staffed all day, determine how long it will take to retrieve a record and deliver it to the user through the interdepartmental mail service. If you have a small center that does not require full-time staffing, you may want to tell users "if we receive your request by 10 A.M., you'll receive the record by 2 P.M." or some similar approach. This system makes it easier for you to group retrievals to-

Exhibit 8-2. Records Request

RECORDS REQUEST	
To be completed by requesting department. Send all copies to Records Center	
Record Title	Dept. Requesting
Record Date	Send To
Box No. (Not Required)	Phone No.
Record Detail	
To be completed by Records Center.	
Requested by: ☐ Phone ☐ Messenger ☐ Mail ☐ Visit	Sent by: ☐ Mail ☐ Messenger ☐ Visit
Searched by	Time Spent
Date Due	Date Returned
Refiled by	
Remarks	
Copy 1: Tickler File Copy 3: On Out Card Copy 2: On Record	

gether, although, of course, if there's an emergency, someone will need to make a special trip to the records center.

Sometimes, even in the best managed records centers, a record cannot be found. When this situation occurs, return one copy of the form to the requester. In the "remarks" section, explain what steps were taken to search for the record.

Keep track of what records were not located because this is an important indicator of the center's efficiency. The formula to use is:

$$\frac{\text{Number of records not found}}{\text{Number of records searched for}}$$

Calculate this ratio as a percentage. If the ratio is .5 percent or less, the center is doing an excellent job of locating records. If the ratio is over 3 percent, you have a definite problem.

To determine the cause of the problem, you'll need to analyze some information about the records that were not found. If most of the records not found were requested by a particular department, investigate that department's record-keeping practices. Perhaps the records were not complete when sent to the center, perhaps the boxes were labeled inaccurately, or perhaps the filing procedures were faulty.

If most of the missing records were searched for by the same individual in the records center, he or she may not be looking diligently enough. For example, if the file is not under the year it was supposed to be, were the years before and after checked? If it's a file on an individual, were other spellings of the name checked? And so on. Retrieval can be a good test of one's detective skills.

Destruction of Records

An important part of the records center's responsibilities is the destruction of records whose retention period has expired. When records are due for the destruction, you should notify the department head responsible for the records using a memo similar to this:

The following records are due for destruction in accordance with Knightly, Inc.'s retention schedule. Please notify me by [date 30 days later] of any records that should not be destroyed and the reason why. If I do not hear from you by [same date], the records will be destroyed.

Since destroying the records is simply complying with company policy, you don't need a departmental signature to authorize destruction. If records are not to be destroyed, that is a deviation from the policy and a legitimate reason should be supplied. Examples of such reasons might be that the record is needed for litigation or for an audit. Destruction should *not* be postponed because the records "might" be needed later or "just in case." Postponing destruction without a valid business reason can invalidate your retention policy and cause problems in case of litigation.

Since a department head may not always be aware of a pending lawsuit or audit, it's a prudent practice to send the legal and tax department a list of all records due for destruction. As with the department heads, destruction will proceed on schedule unless you are notified to the contrary within thirty days.

If the records to be destroyed are confidential, they need to be disposed of in a manner that prevents their reconstruction. Some recyclers will accept sealed cartons and pulp them as is. If this option is available, it's the most desirable one. Of course, nonconfidential wastepaper should be recycled whenever possible.

If confidential recycling isn't available, shredding the records is the next best alternative. Shredders are available in a wide range of models from small units that fit on top of wastebaskets to heavy-duty industrial models. The narrower the shred, the more difficult reconstruction of the records will be. Crosscut shredders (units that cut the paper in both directions) make reconstruction virtually impossible, although the shredding process is considerably slower than straight-cut shredders. After the paper is shredded, it can be recycled.

If you decide to purchase a shredder, measure the volume of records to be destroyed. The most common error in shredder selection is buying a model that is not powerful or fast enough to handle the volume of records to be destroyed.

If you don't choose to destroy the confidential records in house, there are bonded services that will pick up and destroy the records for you. Some services have trucks equipped with shredders and actually destroy the records at your premises. Others shred the records at their facility. If you use such a service, have your contract specify that a member of your staff or your company's security department can, without advance notice, accompany the supplier from the time the records are picked up until they are destroyed. While most such services are extremely reliable, there are exceptions, and you want to be sure your records are properly destroyed.

By now, you may be wondering if this concern about records destruction is a rather paranoid reaction. Well, clients of mine find people searching through their garbage. These companies are in highly competitive industries such as biotechnology and software development, and people are looking for information that might give them an edge either competitively or in terms of the company's stock. Also, your files contain a great deal of confidential information about customers and employees. If these individuals' privacy is violated, they might take legal action against your company.

The secure destruction of records is also an issue in the office. Many of my clients have metal waste bins with locked lids strategically located throughout the company. Paper to be destroyed confidentially is inserted in the slots at the top of the containers. The bins are periodically removed so their contents can be shredded. Be sure to place such containers near photocopiers and printers. How often have you made a poor quality copy of a critical document or printed a copy with an error and just thrown it in the wastebasket?

Two methods of destroying confidential records I normally avoid are incineration and landfills. Unless an elaborate incinerator with air purifiers is used, burning records creates pollution. Also, unless the incineration is very thorough, some records may not be totally destroyed. As far as landfills are concerned, while records eventually decompose, this is a lengthy process and we already have a problem with waste disposal in this country. Moreover, the records could be unearthed.

Cost Analysis

As part of the discussion of records center procedures, I've addressed two measures of quality: the accuracy of the retrieval process and the speed with which records are delivered to the requester. A third measure is the cost effectiveness of the services provided.

I believe in charging users back for records storage. I've found it to be a great motivator for shortening retention periods. If the cost of storing records is in your budget, all too many departments will insist their records are permanent. If the cost is in their budget, they suddenly realize the records may only be needed for three or four years.

As discussed in Chapter 7, if you're using a commercial center, it should be able to break out your bill by department so you can charge each one back for its storage. If you're operating an in-house center, you'll have to determine your costs. Of course, you should do this even if you aren't charging users back. You need to know what your in-house storage costs are and if an in-house operation is more cost effective than using a commercial center.

Typical expenses for an in-house center are:

- Rent or depreciation on the building
- Depreciation or lease payments on the center equipment
- Staff (be sure to include fringe benefits and any temporary help who may be used during peak periods; if your staff only works in the records center part time, prorate the cost accordingly)
- Cartons and other supplies
- Data processing costs
- Telephone and utilities
- Insurance
- Security
- Transportation if the center is located off-site

If your center is not a separate building but a room or two in a larger building, it may not be worth your while to break out some of these costs, such as security and insurance, separately. Use your judgment here and focus on those costs that are incurred only because you have a records center.

After you've totaled all the costs, subtract any recycling income received by the center to obtain the net operating cost. Because you're not operating a commercial facility, there's no point in developing an elaborate pricing strategy for users. If you simply divide the annual net operating cost by the number of boxes in storage, you'll come up with an average cost per box per year to charge users. Since one standard size box is slightly over one cubic foot, this is also approximately your cost per cubic foot.

Keep in mind that your cost to the user includes shelving, indexing, and retrieving the box. Therefore, even if your charge is slightly higher than a commercial center's annual storage fee for a box, you are really less costly.

When setting your fee schedule, you may want to charge separately for cartons. One of my clients noticed that users were requesting large amounts of boxes, but the boxes weren't coming back to the records center. Apparently some unscrupulous individuals had decided that the records center was an excellent source of "free" cartons for moves and other personal activities. Charging users for boxes at the time they request them has eliminated the problem.

Special Problems

To complete our discussion of records center operations, we need to address two situations not of the records manager's making that can complicate his or her life enormously: acquisitions and "inheritances."

Coping With an Acquisition

As mentioned in Chapter 6, when your company acquires another company, it often acquires its records. If possible, this situation should be addressed before the records arrive at your company. It's best if personnel from your company go to the acquired company and supervise the boxing, labeling, and shipping of the records to be transferred.

Here's why: In some cases I've known, the employees of the acquired company were being laid off. Not surprisingly, they were unhappy about the acquisition. As a result, records were mislabeled and, in general, placed in as much as disorder as possible. Also many duplicate and unnecessary items were boxed and shipped. In each instance, cleaning up the mess was costly and time consuming for the acquiring company.

Once the records come into your possession, they'll need to be categorized according to your retention schedule whenever possible. You'll probably need assistance in classification from other departments, especially finance (many of the records will undoubtedly be accounting records).

When there is no match with the retention schedule, appropriate department heads at your company, together with tax and legal input, will need to set retentions. You will undoubtedly find that many of the records are already past their retention and can be disposed of.

Keep a separate listing of the records acquired, their disposition, and the reason why. Then, if litigation should occur, your company is protected from the accusation of selective destruction of records.

Bringing Order Out of Disorder

Another common problem for records managers is inheriting a warehouse, closet, or storage room full of inactive records that are unindexed and in no particular order. This is a common situation when the company has not had a formal records management program.

Your first step should be to declare a moratorium on any more records going into the area. Don't let the problem get any worse than it already is.

Next, get the records physically organized by major subject category (i.e., accounting, marketing, human resources, etc.). Then contact each department with records in the area and ask them to appoint a team to work with you on the cleanup process. The team should include one or more managers and one or more support staff.

I usually begin with the financial records because that's normally the largest category. Set up a day for the team to come to the records center, and suggest that they dress casually since even the best run records center is still a warehouse and less than immaculate. If you're using a commercial center, arrange ahead of time for an on-site workroom and specify which boxes should be pulled and brought to the room for review.

The responsibility of the manager(s) is to review the records, using the retention schedule as a guide, and to determine which can be disposed of and which must be kept. The support staff's job is to rebox the records that must be kept and complete the transfer forms so that the boxes can be entered into the system correctly.

You may find a few surprises as the "housecleaning" progresses. One records manager discovered a copy of the divorce proceedings for another manager! If you do find personal records such as that, ship them back to the appropriate individual immediately with a polite note explaining that you're sure these documents were sent to the records center by mistake.

You'll also probably find a number of records that aren't on the retention schedule because they are no longer created. The department manager should evaluate the records and make a decision as to whether they need to be kept.

Admittedly, this is a less than pleasant task. However, it is a one-time event since the new system and index make it unnecessary in the future. If departments resist assisting you or maintain they don't have the time, point out to management what it's costing to store the records. A few photographs of the chaos also help.

And if someone absolutely refuses to come to the records, then let the records come to him or her. I did this with one recalcitrant department manager. We started shipping him three boxes a week and refused to accept them back into the records center until they were properly boxed and labeled. After a couple of weeks, he "found time" to come review his boxes.

Blow Your Own Horn!

Once you have the records center properly organized, have an open house. Invite people to come see the facility. It will do a great deal to build their confidence in using the records center. If you have some interesting archival documents, set them up in a display as part of the open house. People enjoy seeing old photographs, documents, and other memorabilia. If you have a computerized indexing system, give demonstrations of it. And pat yourself on the back—it's no small achievement to have developed a first-rate records center.

9

Vital Records: Your Organization's Lifeblood

The destruction of vital records in a disaster can cost an organization large amounts of time and money through lost business, time spent re-creating information that was destroyed, tax-related issues that cannot be proved, patent rights that cannot be defended, insurance claims that cannot be supported, and so on. Disasters can range in scope from a broken pipe or a computer system breakdown to hurricanes, earthquakes, floods, and tornadoes. In addition to natural disasters, the organization may be the victim of sabotage or other malicious actions by individuals or groups.

Consequently, *every* organization—large or small—needs a vital records program to protect essential information from destruction. In fact, small companies are often more vulnerable than large ones because all their records and operations may be at one site. With large organizations, the destruction of one location will normally not put the company out of business. Also, duplicate copies of some vital records are usually kept at more than one site through routine business practices. However, without a vital records program, even a large multilocation company can have its operations severely hampered by a disaster or experience a significant financial loss.

Many organizations have a false sense of security because they have installed a "disaster recovery" program. While the term "disaster recovery" can be defined several ways, for most companies, it means a program to get the computer system up and running again after a disaster. As part of such a program, backup copies of all critical computer media are stored off-site and arrangements are made for the use of backup hardware if a disaster occurs.

While disaster recovery is essential, many records necessary to the organization's operation may not be on the computer system. Also, I've found that many disaster recovery programs focus on resuming computer operations and do not adequately protect older information that may be essential for tax or legal reasons.

If your organization has a disaster recovery program that only focuses on resuming computer operations, either the program's scope needs to be broadened to include all vital records, regardless of media, or it needs to be integrated with a vital records program. If no disaster recovery program exists, one needs to be developed in conjunction with a vital records program.

This is an area where the records manager and the systems staff need to work closely together. In addition, the organization needs to consider also the human aspects of a disaster (notifying employees, assigning responsibilities, dealing with the possibility of injured personnel, etc.) and the physical aspects (where business will be conducted if the building is destroyed, rebuilding the facility, etc.). As you can see, the project assumes enormous proportions.

In this book, the focus is limited to the records manager's role in the process. This role typically includes coordination with the systems department's disaster recovery plan, protection of vital records that are not on the computer system, and participation in development of the overall plan for resuming operations after a disaster.

The Program

Getting Management Support

Most records managers find the vital records program the "toughest sell" of all. Organizations give lip service to the idea, but they don't want to spend the money needed to implement a program. And, no doubt about it, a vital records program costs money. Key records have to be duplicated and stored off-site. The program's only monetary return is if a disaster occurs. Then it may save the business.

The best approach I've found is to sell the program as insurance. I always point out that the organization wouldn't think of not carrying insurance on its buildings, equipment, or key personnel. Critical information can be just as important. The vital records program is the equivalent of insurance for that information.

If you're still encountering resistance, a good time to raise the issue again is after a disaster has occurred. For example, a number of organizations in California instituted vital records programs after the recent major earthquakes. The Oklahoma City bombing caused many government agencies to reassess their vital records programs. Or if a company in your area recently has had its operations disrupted due to a fire, this may be a good time to remind senior management "it could happen to us."

Developing Your Definition of Vital Records

After you've obtained approval for the program, the next step is defining the term "vital records." The quick, superficial definition is "those records needed to continue or resume operations in the event of a disaster." That definition includes most but not all vital records. For example, the company's employee pension records aren't necessary to resume its operations, yet they are considered vital because they represent a legal commitment the company has made and must fulfill. So let's expand our definition to include also those records needed to protect:

- The rights of employees and customers
- The equity of the business's owners (i.e., the stockholders, partners, proprietor, or even the public—in the case of the government)
- The organization's legal and financial status

Now we have a comprehensive general definition of vital records. Each different type of organization has to refine this definition further on the basis of its own business. For example, a manufacturing company would consider vital those engineering drawings and specifications necessary to produce its products. A hospital's vital records would include its patients' medical files, and a bank's would include the status of each depositor's account.

Although organizations have these unique needs, certain gen-

eral categories are usually vital. We can expand our basic definition to include these categories. For example, to continue or
resume operations and to meet customer needs, the organization
should protect records that:

- Identify fixed assets (the company's land, buildings, plants,
  and equipment) and determine their value. This information
  is essential for filing an insurance claim, as well as for resuming operations.
- Identify and, when possible, fulfill existing commitments
  to customers.
- Rebuild facilities (when appropriate).
- Develop new business.
- Identify the nature and value of inventory.
- Resume computer system operations and telecommunications.

To ensure the rights of employees, the organization should
protect records that:

- State salaries and benefits due employees and former employees (pension, vacation, insurance, etc.).
- State any other corporate commitments to employees, such
  as union contracts.

To safeguard legal, financial, and shareholder interests, the organization should protect records that:

- Determine receivables (what customers and others owe the
  company). This is critical as a credit and collection problem
  often occurs after a disaster. Customers sometimes hope
  their records were destroyed and the company will be unaware of the money owed it.
- Determine liabilities (what the company owes to others).
  Yes, the company's creditors will remind it of its debts, but
  you want to be sure the reminders are accurate.
- Identify the locations and amounts of cash and securities
  owned by the company, as well as protecting any deeds,
  notes, or negotiable securities in the organization's possession.

- Establish and defend the organization's tax position.
- Identify shareholders and their stock holdings.
- Meet all legal requirements for establishing the corporate status (documentation required by federal and state agencies such as the Securities and Exchange Commission).
- Protect intangible assets such as patents and trademarks.

Many of the records on the list can be protected through the disaster recovery system (e.g., payroll records). Vital records that are not computer generated include:

- Contracts, leases, license and franchise agreements, and other such documents where a signature is critical. (Note: be selective. A contract for snow removal is probably not vital, but a contract to build a new plant would be.)
- Laboratory notebooks and other research data. (Some research data will be computer generated, but handwritten lab notebooks are usually the pivotal document.)
- Engineering drawings, blueprints, and the like. (Newer drawings are usually on the computer system, but older ones may not be.)
- Product formulas and production specifications.
- Insurance policies.
- Articles of incorporation, bylaws, and board minutes.
- Patents, trademarks, copyrights, and so on.
- Deeds and titles to property.

Identifying Your Vital Records

Unless your company is a very small "mom and pop" type business, no one person will have a broad enough knowledge of all records and systems to identify the vital records. You will need a committee to make the identification. It's best if the committee members are fairly high-level managers. If you ask a department head which of his or her records are vital, the answer usually is "all of them." The department head views those records as being essential to the department's work—which is not the same as being essential to the company's existence. A committee composed of senior staff is usually more selective.

Although the exact membership of the committee will vary from company to company, typically it should include:

The records manager
Corporate legal counsel
The controller or other key finance department member
The individual in the systems area responsible for the disaster recovery program
The personnel or human resources manager
Internal auditor
Security director
Representatives from key operational areas such as sales/marketing, operations/production, research, and engineering

The individuals on the committee should (1) be very familiar with their areas and the records in those areas, and (2) be willing and able to devote some time to the program until it's operational. A good approach is to have the committee meet regularly—perhaps every two weeks—until all vital records are identified and a plan for their protection is established.

While this task may sound overwhelming, you've already done much of the legwork if you have a retention schedule. Since the schedule lists all of the company's records, it's a logical starting point.

First, nonessential records are eliminated. Next, those records that have essential data but can be re-created are eliminated. For example, I-9 immigration forms can be redone; hence, they are not vital. Also identify all situations where the necessary information is or can be protected through computer system backups. Finally, reevaluate those records remaining on the list to ensure that they are vital. (By the way, don't forget that the vital records schedule and the disaster recovery program *are* vital records!)

Preparing the vital records schedule from the retention schedule ensures that you don't overlook any critical record categories. In screening the records, a simple but effective approach is for the committee to ask two questions:

1. What would we be unable to do if this record were destroyed?

2. How critical is our inability to do this? In other words, what is the impact on our organization?

Screening thoroughly is important because protecting records from accidental destruction is costly. To get the maximum benefit from the investment, it's important that only essential records be protected.

Protecting the Vital Records

After the organization's vital records are identified, the committee must select an appropriate way to protect them. Most businesses use a combination of strategies, depending on the record category and its normal usage patterns. The goal is to use the simplest, most economical method that fits the circumstances. The choices are:

- Existing dispersal
- Duplicating the record
- Protecting the original

Existing Dispersal

"Existing dispersal" is the formal title for the vital records protection you already have. As a normal part of doing business, copies of a record may be kept at more than one location. For example, if both a branch office and corporate headquarters maintain a copy of a record, it would be protected.

As a corollary to existing dispersal within the company, when copies of your organization's vital records are kept by others outside the company, those records may—under certain circumstances—be considered protected. The qualifier here is that the outside group's interests are compatible with your organization's. For example, if an outside law firm that does work for your company has copies of key litigation files, those records would be protected. However, your creditors' copies of records of your liabilities would not provide protection as their interests are not the same as your company's. And I would be leery of assuming that a record is protected because it has been filed with a government agency. I've known of too many instances where the agency either could not or would not provide a copy of the record.

If you are depending on an outside organization for protection, check its retention practices to ensure that the records are being maintained for as long as you would need them and that the records would be available to you.

Duplicating the Record

For the vast majority of vital records, duplication is the only viable approach. With this system, the record is duplicated and the duplicate copy stored off-site. If the records are on computer-readable media, a backup copy of the medium is stored off-site. Other alternatives are microfilming the records or, if there are only a few documents, photocopying them.

If the records are microfilmed, store the original film off-site in a climate controlled location and keep a working copy of the film in the office. Then, if a disaster occurs, you'll be able to make another first-generation copy from the original. (With film, you lose quality with each generation, just as photocopies of photocopies are not as clear as photocopies of originals.) In fact, because duplicating microfilm is so inexpensive (the major expense is the filming), it makes sense to make a copy of any film and store the original off-site. (I discuss microfilming in more detail in Chapter 11.)

Protecting the Original

In some very limited circumstances, a microfilm copy of the original may not be legally acceptable (e.g., securities or negotiable instruments). Or the original document may be added to daily, as a laboratory notebook that is not yet complete. In these cases, the original record needs to be protected.

This can be done by storing the record in a vault or fire-resistant file cabinet. If you are going to invest in such equipment, you need to understand its benefits and its limitations.

First of all, the equipment is expensive. A fire-resistant file cabinet may cost $1,000 or more. Therefore, you want to use them selectively, not for all vital records. Secondly, they are heavy. A fire-resistant file cabinet typically weighs over 500 pounds, and, of course, vaults and safes are much heavier. Hence, you'll have to consider the floor's ability to tolerate the weight. Finally, consider how quickly you'll need to access the records after the disaster. The building may not be safe to enter for days or even weeks after the disaster.

On the other hand, properly selected equipment can provide significant protection. Such equipment is tested by Underwriters Laboratories (UL) and rated both for temperature and time. The temperature rating means that the cabinet's interior should not go above a certain temperature when the exterior is exposed to intense heat. If the equipment has a 350°F limit, it will protect paper records. Equipment with a 150°F limit will protect magnetic tape, microfilm, and other photographic records.

The time limit rating is the length of time the equipment can be exposed to the intense heat without its contents reaching the specified temperature. Most fire-resistant file cabinets are one hour rated, while safes and vaults are typically rated for four hours.

A practical tip here—if anyone tells you their records are protected in fire-resistant cabinets, ask to see the equipment. I remember vividly the bank mortgage staff member who assured me all the original signed notes were in "fireproof files." In fact, the notes were in standard four drawer file cabinets which conduct heat beautifully and would have provided no protection. If you're not sure about a piece of equipment, look for the rating plate that is usually found inside the top drawer.

The Vital Records Center

The Facility

By now, you've probably concluded that the majority of your vital records will be protected by storing a duplicate copy off-site. The next question is "Where?"

While a few very large corporations have found it practical to build their own vital records centers, most organizations find it more practical to use a commercial facility.

When selecting a facility, all of the considerations discussed in Chapter 7 for commercial records centers apply. Any vital records storage facility should also meet the following guidelines:

▪ Twenty-four-hour climate control with a temperature of approximately 20°C or 68°F and a relative humidity of 30–40%. Consistent climate control is essential to preserve microfilm and magnetic media. (Note: Most offices are not climate controlled because constant temperature is not maintained over the weekends.)

▪ A location far enough away that the same disaster will not destroy both it and your site. Seventy-five miles along the Atlantic coast in a hurricane zone won't do it. On the other hand, there's no point in a New York company using a vital records facility in Utah. You need to consider how quickly you can gain access to the records if a disaster occurs.

Storage Media

Vital records should be stored on a medium that will last as long as the records are needed. When properly filmed, processed, and stored, microfilm can last for 500 years. Equipment to read microfilm is and will continue to be readily available. Acid-free paper has a life expectancy of over 300 years. Regular office paper may be expected to last 20 to 30 years. With electronic storage media, the issue is the ongoing availability of equipment and software to access the information. For this reason, these records should be reviewed every 3 years and, if necessary, transferred to later versions of the media and/or software.

The Vital Records Schedule

After all the decisions have been made as to what records are to be protected, how this is to be done, and where the records will be kept, this information needs to be documented.

Since only a small percentage of a company's records are vital, this schedule will be much shorter than the retention schedule. Just as with the retention schedule, the easiest approach is to create a database and print out the schedule.

Typical database fields are:

Record title—this should match the title on the retention schedule. It's also a good idea to indicate on the retention schedule if a record is vital.

Method of protection—existing dispersal, microfilming, computer-readable media backup, etc.

Location of copies

Frequency of deposit—how much data can you afford to lose? With magnetic media, the backup is usually daily. However, with paper records, this is not usually practical. For example, with laboratory notebooks, the decision might be to film or electronically image them after completion and to store them in a fire-resistant file until they are completed.

Department responsible for making the deposit—if this isn't the records management department, be sure to have adequate safeguards to ensure records are copied and deposited off-site on schedule.

Retention—sometimes a record is not classified as "vital" for its entire life span, and as a result, the retention schedule value may not be appropriate here.

Testing and Updating the Program

Just as your company holds (or should hold) periodic fire drills, so should it also test the vital records/disaster recovery programs to ensure that they will function properly if a disaster occurs. The first step in the test is picking a team of employees who would have to reconstruct operations in the event of a disaster. The employees are then given a set of information needs the organization would have after the disaster. Using only the protected records, the employees must demonstrate that they can recreate the data and provide the appropriate information.

Here are some sample test problems:

- Continue paying employees on time and making all proper payroll deductions.
- Prepare a current inventory of all company assets.
- Send revised shipping instructions to vendors with outstanding orders.
- Prepare an insurance claim for a particular location. (You may want to discuss with the insurance company to determine what kind of documentation it needs to honor the claim.)

- Collect all information needed to resume manufacture of a particular product or to resume service in a certain area.

Most organizations that have a program and test it do so annually. The consensus is that testing is one of the most valuable steps in the process. I've yet to find a company that did not discover "holes" in its program when the test was done. Tests also keep employees alert and prepared to cope with a crisis.

Just like the retention schedule, the vital records program should be revised annually. Any new record categories created in the past year should be reviewed to determine if they are vital. Records currently classified as vital should be assessed to see if they still are. Doing the revision after the annual test is a good approach because you can correct any flaws that the test revealed.

What If a Disaster Does Occur?

Hopefully you'll never find out how well the program works; however, disasters do happen. Documentation of the vital records/ disaster recovery program should be readily obtainable by appropriate staff members at any time. Some organizations have key employees keep a copy of the disaster recovery manual at their homes. Others maintain copies at a secure commercial records facility with twenty-four-hour access.

While the program should have protected all essential records, there will be other records you would like to recover, as well as records that will be totally destroyed.

Your first priority is salvaging recoverable records. A number of professional companies specialize in saving records that have been damaged by water or other causes. Your microfilm or computer systems vendor may be able to recommend someone. Also, most libraries know of companies that specialize in recovering damaged documents. If you have water damaged records, do *not* try to dry them out on your own. Contact a professional. In fact, the wisest approach is to identify qualified professionals now— not after a disaster. Then you'll know whom to call should the worst happen.

Of course, some records will be unrecoverable. In this situation, you want to document as much as possible what these records were. Then if the company should be asked to produce them for litigation or some other purpose, you'll be able to explain why they are not available. For example, one California company's records center was damaged in a mud slide. Records on lower shelves were not recoverable. The records manager took photographs of the damage and used the records center index to prepare a list of the destroyed records.

10

Managing Active Files Effectively

Up to now, I've dealt primarily with inactive records. For all too many organizations, that's where records management stops. Individual departments maintain their active working records any way they wish. This approach can cause major problems. Support staff often develop filing systems they alone understand, so problems arise when they're absent. Several departments may keep unnecessary and costly duplicate files instead of sharing one common set of information. The wrong types of filing equipment may be selected, thus slowing retrieval and wasting both space and money. And finally, when the records go to inactive storage, they may be in an order intelligible only to the original filer—thus complicating retrieval.

These problems arise because many departments (1) do not have the expertise to establish the most effective filing systems and (2) do not regard filing as a priority—at least, not until they can't find a record. Hence, it makes sense to involve professionals—the records management staff—in departmental filing systems.

Uniform Filing Systems

One way to reduce departmental filing problems is to establish a uniform filing system. Such a system superimposes a "master" subject filing system on all of the organization's records. A uniform filing system is virtually a "must" when files are centralized in one area because it greatly simplifies retrieval, groups related records together, and eliminates the accidental storage of duplicate records.

Uniform filing systems can also be used effectively when departments maintain their own files. In this scenario, each department classifies and maintains its records according to the uniform system, thus saving the time otherwise spent in designing its own system. If the organization decides later to centralize its files, the conversion process will be much easier.

A uniform system makes it possible to locate quickly any file, regardless of where it is kept. It eliminates "miscellaneous" files as every document has a place within the system. And it simplifies training because employees only have to learn one filing system.

However, developing a uniform system requires significant amounts of time and energy. Because different organizations have different types of records, the subject categories for classifying these records also vary. As a result, you'll need to develop a system unique to your organization. Also, if the system is implemented in a decentralized program where individual departments maintain their own files, a monitoring system such as files audits will be necessary to ensure compliance with the program.

Another consideration is initial user resistance to the concept. Departments that are not experiencing major problems with their files may resent having to modify their system. And some individuals even try to use complex filing systems as job security. ("I'm the only person who can find anything; hence, I'm essential.")

To implement an organization-wide system, you will need strong management support. It's usually much easier to implement a uniform system in a small organization (typically fewer than 100 employees) than in a larger one. However, some extremely large organizations, including various branches of the federal government, have successfully implemented uniform systems. In any size organization, the keys to success are simple, clearly defined categories and well-trained filing personnel.

Developing a Uniform System

As a first step, use the data from the records inventory and the retention schedule to select major subject headings for the system. Or, if you prefer, you can combine preparing the retention schedule and the uniform filing system and do both tasks simultaneously.

Choose appropriate alpha codes for each major subject heading. Alpha codes are preferable because, unlike numeric codes, they instantly remind the users of the subjects they represent. Some typical main headings and codes might be:

ADM   Administration
ENG   Engineering
ENV   Environment and Safety
FIN   Finance and Accounting
HUM   Human Resources
INS   Insurance
LEG   Legal
MFG   Manufacturing
MKT   Marketing

These headings do not refer specifically to the records of various departments but rather to all corporate records pertaining to that subject. For example, the finance department will have records on its employees that fall under the human resources category, while the human resources department's budget records would belong in the finance category.

Avoid main subject headings such as "forms," "correspondence," and "reports" that indicate the format of the information rather than its contents. Also, do not link the filing system to account codes or organization charts as these change frequently. If two divisions have manufacturing facilities, both will use the MFG heading for records they have on that subject.

Each subject heading and subheading should have a clear written definition, such as, "Finance and accounting: Records pertaining to all financial and accounting activities, including general accounting, tax, payroll, budget, cash management, and investments." Written definitions ensure that records are properly classified.

Limit the number of main headings because too many headings make it difficult for users to categorize records correctly. As a general rule, the number of main headings should not exceed thirty. I usually find that fifteen or fewer headings are all that are needed.

Next, develop subheadings for each main category. For example, "Finance and accounting" might be subdivided as follows:

FIN 01   General Accounting
FIN 02   Accounts Receivable
FIN 03   Accounts Payable
FIN 04   Treasury and Cash Management
FIN 05   Payroll
FIN 06   Taxes

and so on. . . .

As you develop the system, you will probably note areas that overlap. For example, the company has records on payroll taxes. Your written definition needs to indicate whether they will be found under FIN 05 or FIN 06. (You'd probably use FIN 05 as these records are an integral part of the payroll system and are normally managed by that department.)

Each of the subheadings is divided one more time. For example, FIN 03 (Accounts Payable) might be broken down as follows:

FIN 03-01   Supplier Invoices
FIN 03-02   Employee Expense Reports
FIN 03-03   Accounts Payable Reports

and so on. . . .

Note that with the first two items, we have now reached actual records that would then be filed in whatever way is appropriate (invoices by supplier number, for example). The third item, the reports, would then be broken down one more time into the various reports (FIN 03-03-01, FIN 03-03-02, etc.). By the third or fourth breakout, you should have reached actual records categories. If the system involves more than three or four levels of classification, it will become too complicated and records will be categorized incorrectly.

To simplify the classification process, the uniform filing system should be supported by a detailed alphabetic index that lists each record under all of its possible names. For example, the company's federal income tax return might be indexed under "IRS Form 1120," "Federal Income Tax Return," and "Income Tax Return—Federal." Be sure to index all reports and forms by their form or report number as well as by their names.

Here's a sample portion of an index under the letter "I":

I-9 Immigration Forms	HUM 01-03
Insurance Claims	
Health	INS 03-01
Property	INS 03-02
Insurance Policies	
Health	INS 01-01
Property	INS 01-02
Invoices	
Customer	FIN 02-01
Supplier	FIN 03-01

User input is essential for a successful filing system. I usually prepare a draft version based on the inventory data. Then I submit the draft to the users for feedback, make any necessary revisions, and resubmit it. After everyone agrees on the draft, I test the system by converting a limited number of records. The test often reveals areas that need to be corrected or situations that had not been foreseen.

Of course, training is needed for all individuals who will be using the system. And to ensure consistency throughout the organization, all changes to the system must be cleared through the records management area.

Uniform Filing on the Departmental Level

All of the guidelines just discussed can also be applied on a smaller scale to developing a subject filing system for an individual department's records. For example, if you were developing a uniform filing system for just the legal department, some main headings might be:

CON	Contracts
FIN	Finance
LTG	Litigation
PAT	Patents
SHR	Shareholder Records and Investor Relations

While the finance heading might seem out of place, the legal department will have a limited number of financial records: invoices, budgets, and the like.

It is easier to prepare a departmental system than an organization-wide system since you will have fewer record categories to organize and you only need one group's "buy-in" for the project. However, it will be more difficult to match up record categories because different departments will assign different codes to the same record. For example, both the legal department and the human resources department may maintain litigation files. For the legal department, litigation would be the major subject heading, while legal would probably be the major heading for human resources.

Filing Individual Record Categories

A uniform filing system imposes an overall order on records. A separate issue is determining the best way to file individual records categories such as "employee personnel files," "litigation files," "sales orders," and so on. No one filing system is appropriate for all categories. Therefore, the records manager must choose the best system for each category.

Alphabetical Filing by Name

Filing material alphabetically by name is the oldest, simplest, and most commonly used of all filing systems. Typical applications include personnel files, vendor files, and customer files. The system's primary virtue is its simplicity. No index is needed to find a particular file, and classifying the material to be filed is relatively straightforward.

However, even the simplest system has drawbacks. In an alphabetic system of more than 1,000 files, confusion over a name's proper spelling can make retrieval difficult. The name "Burke," for example, can also be spelled Berk, Berke, Birk, Birke, and Burk. In a small system, finding the correct spelling is relatively easy, but in a large system, searching is time-consuming, costly, and frustrating.

Another common error is misfiling ambiguous first and last names. Is it "Scott Leslie" or "Leslie Scott"? An additional problem is errors due to unclear or nonexistent filing rules. For example, is "R. R. Donnelly & Co." filed at the beginning of the Rs, after "Robert's Plumbing," or in the Ds?* One filing system had files for the company in all three places, because different filers made different decisions.

Some organizations solve these problems by developing their own set of standardized filing rules to cover such situations. However, a simple, more effective solution is to adopt the Association of Records Managers and Administrators' *Alphabetic Filing Rules* as the company standard in this area. The rules have been adopted as standard by the American National Standards Institute (ANSI) and can be obtained from ARMA International for a nominal charge.

Numeric Filing Systems

Because of the potential for confusion with a large alphabetic filing system, many organizations assign unique numbers to individual files. Thus, the hospital files your patient record by a patient number, unique to you, ensuring that your file is not confused with that of another individual with a similar name. Numeric systems do, of course, require an index to cross-reference the number with what it represents.

There are three basic types of numerical filing systems: consecutive, terminal digit, and middle digit.

Consecutive Numeric Filing

Consecutive numeric filing is the simplest of the numeric systems. As the name implies, documents or files are placed in consecutive order according to their assigned number. Such a system works well for fewer than 10,000 files. With larger numbers of files, several problems arise. It is more time consuming to file documents with five digit numbers, and the likelihood of error is sub-

---

*Answer: at the beginning of the Rs.

stantially greater when five digits are filed consecutively instead of four.

Also, since the most recently created files are generally the most frequently referenced, filing activity is greatest at the end of the numeric series. Often, several files personnel need to work in the same area and get in each other's way. Finally, when older files at the front end of the series are retired to storage, the remaining files have to be moved down to make room for the new files at the end.

Terminal Digit Filing

Terminal digit filing was developed to overcome these problems. The terminal digit system is based on the principle of filing "backward" in groups of two or three digits. Each file number is typically divided into three groups. Thus, file 110319 is 11 03 19.

The groups are filed in reverse order. All the files ending in 00 come first, then those ending in 01, then those ending in 02, and so on. Next, the files are grouped by their middle digits, so that all the 00 01s come before the 01 01s. And finally the files are arranged by their first digits so that 11 00 01 would precede 12 00 01, which would come before 13 00 01.

Here's an example of how a group of files in terminal digit order would be arranged:

11	01	00
9	02	00
12	03	00
88	02	01
20	10	01
21	10	01
16	09	02

Although this system may initially sound confusing, once filing personnel are trained, fewer misfiles occur than with a consecutive numbering system. Errors decrease because files personnel are working with groups of two or three digits instead of a long string of five or more digits. To further enhance its effectiveness, terminal digit filing should be used with color coding (discussed later in this chapter).

With a terminal digit system, the newest and presumably most heavily referenced files are spread out throughout the shelves or cabinets instead of concentrated at the end. Consequently, files personnel work uniformly throughout the system, and "traffic jams" are avoided. Also, when older files are pulled for storage or destruction, they are pulled throughout the system, thus eliminating the need to shift files down.

Terminal digit filing is typically used for large, active numeric files such as hospital patient records, insurance policy files, and bank loan files.

Middle Digit Filing

One of terminal digit filing's advantages can also be a disadvantage. Namely, if you want to retrieve 100 consecutively numbered files, you must go to 100 different locations in the filing system. Middle digit filing was designed to eliminate that problem and is used for the same types of files as are terminal digit systems.

Just as the name implies, filing begins with the middle grouping of digits. Then the records are filed by the first group of digits and finally by the last group. Consequently, as the example below shows, files whose middle digits are 00 would be first, then 01, and so on.

1	00	22
1	00	23
12	00	01
5	01	20
6	01	19
6	01	20
16	01	01

Because 100 consecutive files, such as 1 00 00 to 1 00 99, are located together, it is easier to convert a consecutive numeric system to middle digit filing than to terminal digit. When supplemented by color coding, middle digit, like terminal digit, has a low error rate. One disadvantage to the middle digit approach is that filing activity is not spread out as evenly as in a terminal digit system. Also, it may take personnel slightly longer to adjust to a middle digit system than to a terminal digit system because the numeric ordering is somewhat more complex.

Computer Indexing Active Files

If a file needs to be retrieved by more than one identifier, then computer indexing becomes desirable. For example, the legal department might want to computer index contract files by:

- Name of the other party to the contract
- Department within the company involved in the contract
- Date the contract was signed
- Date the contract expires or is up for renewal
- Subject of the contract or what it pertains to
- File location

Such an index makes it simple to locate all contracts that expired in the past year or all contractual commitments made with a particular company. The actual files can be placed in any order that seems desirable, such as alphabetically by name of the other party or by contract number (an identifying number assigned by the legal department and included in the index).

Any standard relational database package can be used to prepare this type of index. And, of course, the records could be maintained on a nonpaper medium such as microfilm or optical disk.

Computer indexing is a valuable tool, but like any such tool it can be misused. Inputing data into the index takes time; hence, the indexing fields should be selected carefully. Indexing files by fields that will not be used is a waste of time and energy.

It is also important to develop a standardized terminology for subject indexing. For example, if the contract's subject is entered as "cleaning and janitorial services" and we search for all contracts pertaining to "building maintenance," we won't find the cleaning contract. Subject indexing is always subjective, but developing a thesaurus of standard terms will help ensure that all relevant documents are found.

Another approach to indexing documents is text search and retrieval. Of course, documents created and stored on a computer can be text searched. Other documents can be scanned using OCR (optical character recognition). Once the text is captured on the computer, it can be searched. This type of indexing is being used increasingly with the document imaging systems discussed in the next chapter.

While it can be extremely effective, there are some potential problems. First, while OCR software is continually improving, scanning errors do occur. A 99 percent accuracy rate still means three to four errors per page. Second, you have to search using the terminology used in the document. For example, if you search under EEO (or equal employment opportunity) and the document refers to "affirmative action" instead, you won't find the document.

Of course, all files do not need computer indexing. If a file only needs to be located by one identifier, simply file it in that order. For example, the company with 800 employees will probably find it easiest to keep the personnel files in alphabetical order by last name. On the other hand, it might be beneficial to computer index job applications and resumes of potential new hires so that they can be searched by the types of positions the individuals might be considered for, as well as by applicant name and date of the application.

To Centralize or Not, That Is the Question

So far, I've discussed various methods for organizing files. A separate issue is whether or not some or all of the organization's active files should be combined in one location and what type of overall control should be applied to active files.

In this chapter the discussion is confined to paper files. In the next chapter I cover imaging systems that can provide an electronic central files. With such systems, users retrieve and view the records on their workstations. This type of system provides many benefits but can be costly.

Decentralization is the most common approach for handling active files. It is also the least desirable. While some departments do an excellent job of maintaining their records, others are less motivated and allow each individual to maintain his or her individual files. This approach can be both costly and inefficient.

First of all, professional staff members such as engineers and scientists usually make very poor filers. I can think of at least three large corporate engineering departments where the filing system was "random," that is, most engineers put the files in their cabinets as the spirit moved them, not even in date sequence or alphabetically. This problem is not unique to engineers. Professional staff are also very expensive filers; support staff will do the same work far better for a far lower cost.

An even greater problem is the fact that information is not shared. In research departments where each scientist maintains separate files, work is often redone unnecessarily because individuals have no way of knowing what studies have already been performed. Also, when an individual leaves, valuable information is often poorly organized or even impossible to locate. It may even have left the organization.

In every research organization I have ever worked with I have found files individuals brought from previous employers. Yes, this does violate the confidentiality agreements these individuals signed, but it does happen. While it is impossible to stop individuals from taking information if they are so inclined, it is possible through centralized systems to ensure at least that your organization also retains possession of the information.

Therefore, any controls you can implement for active records will benefit the organization. I'll first cover how a centralized system works and then discuss ways of ensuring the success of centralization.

A Typical Central Files Program

With a central files program, all active files except those being created or used at that time are kept in one or more central file rooms. These rooms function as libraries, with records being checked out to users and follow-ups conducted if the records are not returned on time.

Central files provide the following advantages:

- A thorough knowledge, and consequently a more effective use, of the information kept within the organization.
- Fewer misfiles and lost records because all filing and retrieval is done by professionals whose sole job is operating the file room.
- More efficient use of office space through the elimination of duplicate records and the use of space efficient high-density filing equipment (to be discussed later in this chapter).
- More effective use of clerical staff through the elimination of time spent filing duplicates.
- Improved compliance with the retention schedule because the central files staff ensures that records are sent to storage or disposed of on schedule.

With such an impressive list of benefits, you might wonder why every organization doesn't adopt a central files system. There are two main difficulties. One is physical impracticality. The way a building is constructed may mean that there is no space that can be used for central file area. Also if a company's facilities are spread over a wide area, centralizing active records in one location is impractical and inefficient. Such a company might consider a number of central file areas, each serving the users at a particular site.

The second and greater difficulty is user resistance. As already discussed, most users want *their* records at *their* fingertips. Users tend to forget that the records belong to the organization and think of them as their personal property.

Therefore, establishing a central files system usually must be mandated by senior management. And, increasingly, senior management is insisting on at least some centralization to protect information, ensure its accessibility, and conserve space.

However, I don't want to give you the impression of creating a records dictatorship. Having installed a number of central file rooms, I can assure you that while there is initial resistance, before the first year's anniversary, most users are extolling the virtues of central files and wondering how they ever got along without the program.

Making Central Files a Success

Following a few simple guidelines will help defuse user resistance and make the program a success. These include:

1. *Locate the central files area(s) to be convenient for users.* If people have to walk half a mile or go down five floors to retrieve their records, they're going to be reluctant to send their files to a central location. Good locations are near the cafeteria, the rest rooms, or the coffee pot since most individuals go there frequently.

2. *Be aware that the central files concept is most readily accepted in organizations that already have successful records management programs in other areas.* For example, if users have confidence in the records center for storing inactive records, they are more likely to trust their active records to central files.

3. *Make sure the program has strong senior management support.* Corporate policy should require user compliance with the program. In addition to policy, visible support from top management helps. At one company, the CEO asked that his files be inventoried and incorporated into the central files system first. Of course, other managers were quick to follow his example.

4. *Establish the program gradually.* Bring one group of records into the files area at a time. Otherwise, you'll have confusion and frustrated users. It's also a good idea to start with departments or groups who are most receptive to the program. Make the highly resistant groups the last ones you merge into the system. By then, they'll see that the program is working smoothly, and it will be harder for them to oppose it.

5. *Communicate with the users.* Get user input on procedures for submitting records, retrieving them, and so on. Prepare a booklet ("Welcome to Central Files!") that explains the procedures, hours of operation, and the like. After the room is operational, invite everyone to an open house. (Cookies or other "goodies" will encourage people to come.) Seeing a well-organized facility does much to reduce resistance. You may also want to attend departmental staff meetings to explain the operation and answer any questions.

6. *Do not allow users to retrieve or refile records.* Even users with the best intentions will not complete out cards (see later in this chapter)—either because they forget or because they're in a hurry. Once files are removed without the knowledge of the central files personnel, the integrity of the files is destroyed. Once records thought to be in central files are found missing, users will cease to trust the operation and maintain their own duplicate files. And if users refile, misfiles will increase dramatically.

7. *Train central files staff to be customer-service oriented.* The staff must respond quickly to critical requests and be courteous at all times. While procedures must be enforced, this can be done pleasantly.

8. *Either follow up on checked out records or don't check out records.* If you don't follow up on checked out documents, at some point you'll go to retrieve a record and find out it was checked out a year ago, the person that had it left six months ago, and now no one knows where it is.

The other alternative is not to allow originals to leave the room. In this scenario, small work areas are available in the room for users to reference documents. When users need to remove records, they receive a photocopy. While this process may seem cumbersome, if the documents are essential to the organization, it's a wise precaution. For example, many pharmaceutical companies follow this practice with documents that must be available for regulatory agencies. If you do opt for the photocopying approach, identify the copies as duplicates. This may be done by using colored paper or paper that has the word "copy" screened on it.

9. *Make sure file room hours are adequate for user needs.* Organizations on "flex-time" often stagger file room staffing and lunch hours so that the room is open for a wide range of hours such as 7:30 A.M. to 6:00 P.M. And if records may be needed after hours in an emergency, have a procedure for reaching records staff at home to retrieve the records. (Don't be unduly nervous about this. I've found that emergency retrievals are virtually nonexistent, but users feel greatly comforted by the fact that an emergency procedure exists.)

10. *Develop simple procedures for submitting documents for filing and for checking out records.* I usually develop simple forms that us-

ers can attach to documents being submitted. By using check boxes to indicate the various types of documents, you can greatly reduce the amount of writing needed on the form. For high-volume users, you may want to preprint their names and departments on the form. Save these forms as a record of the documents that have been submitted for filing. Sometimes users think they have submitted documents when they haven't. They then accuse central files of losing the records. Being able to show what files were actually received can reduce many problems.

11. *Consider carefully whether highly confidential records should be kept in central files.* Many organizations exclude legal, payroll, and personnel records from central files, preferring to have "mini" central files in those areas. With research files, some organizations limit access by topic so that only individuals working on a particular project can access its files.

12. *Consider using central files selectively.* The selective approach means that files referenced by several departments, such as a bank's mortgage files, or that are essential to the organization's existence, such as a pharmaceutical company's clinical study files and Food and Drug Administration submissions, are kept in central files. Records primarily of interest to one department are maintained in that department.

Other organizations opt for departmental central files maintained by the support staff of that department. However, the support staff usually has many duties other than filing, and it is more difficult to maintain control in such situations.

Filing Equipment

Whether or not you centralize files, it is important to select the right type of filing equipment for each situation. If at all possible, I recommend that *all* purchases of filing equipment be approved by the records manager. This practice prevents waste. Before approving any request, the records manager checks to make sure the department is in compliance with the retention schedule. Many departments buy unnecessary equipment simply because no one has purged the files. The records manager's approval also ensures that the most appropriate equipment is selected. Factors to consider when selecting equipment include:

Access frequency and retrieval speed. Drawer filing systems are slower than shelf systems. If records are accessed heavily, fast retrieval is a key factor. Also, with some types of equipment, all of the records are not physically available at the same time. If extremely rapid retrieval is needed, this may be a problem.

Filing features. What size and type are the records—legal size, letter size, computer printouts, three-ring binders? Does the entire file folder need to be pulled or just selected items from it?

You should find your need for legal size file cabinets diminishing. ARMA International's Project ELF (Eliminate Legal Files) has been quite successful in convincing courts to require materials on letter size paper rather than legal size. Most of the legal size cabinets I see at clients are filled with letter size materials. Since legal size cabinets and filing supplies cost more and consume more space, use them only when necessary.

While legal size paper is on the way out, metric or A4 paper is on the way in. "Letter size" paper is not the norm in the rest of the world. Virtually all other countries use A4 paper, which is slightly narrower than 8 ½-by-11-inch paper and about two-thirds of an inch the longer. The additional length causes the filing problem. Unfortunately, most U.S. manufacturers of filing equipment and supplies have not yet addressed this issue. If you can purchase equipment designed for A4 documents, I would strongly encourage you to do so. Even if the United States does not shift to metric paper, in this global economy your organization is sure to receive a steadily increasing number of A4 documents.

Space requirements. Must the equipment fit in a particular area?

Space cost versus equipment cost. If you're located in a "high-rent district," more expensive equipment that can hold a large amount of records in a small space may be cost justified.

Building structure. Most high density filing equipment requires reinforced floors.

Security. How confidential are the records? Filing equipment locks provide limited security. Often a number of cabinets can be opened with the same key. Obtaining duplicate keys is usually easy to do. Also, such locks can be "popped open" fairly easily. If the files need to be really secure, they should be kept in a room that is locked when unattended.

Fire protection. As discussed in Chapter 9, standard filing cabinets do not provide fire protection. If records are vital, they will need some form of extra protection.

Mobility. Some types of filing equipment are built-in and costly to move.

System growth. Be sure that the system will meet future needs as well as present criteria.

Keeping these criteria in mind, consider the various types of filing equipment.

Vertical File Cabinets

The vertical file cabinet is the oldest filing equipment option. In recent years, it's been maligned, primarily because it's been misused. The vertical file is still a good choice for storing records in individual offices or small departments. However, if more than four vertical file cabinets are needed in an area, you should consider other options, because at that point the cabinets are not space efficient.

Vertical files require 44 inches of aisle space for pulling out drawers. Five-drawer cabinets provide more filing capacity for the same amount of floor space as four-drawer cabinets. However, unless your filing team is composed of professional basketball players, you may find that the staff has difficulty seeing into the top drawer.

Since a drawer must be opened, retrieval and filing are relatively slow. Also, only one person can use a file cabinet at a time. However, documents can be added to or removed from a folder without the user's removing the entire folder from the cabinet.

Lateral Filing Cabinets

Lateral cabinets are more attractive than vertical cabinets and only require 30 inches of aisle space. Laterals do, of course, require more wall space. Records may be filed either sideways or front to back as in a vertical file. Like vertical files, lateral cabinets are best suited for individual offices and small departmental records collections.

Since laterals are a drawer system, the same limitations as to access and retrieval speeds apply as with vertical cabinets. Also five-drawer cabinets pose the same retrieval problems for shorter personnel.

Open-Shelf Filing

Shelf filing systems provide faster retrieval than drawer systems and permit simultaneous multiple-user access. Because users do not have to look down into a drawer, the systems can be higher than drawer units, thus adding filing capacity. Additional space is conserved since drawers do not have to be pulled out. Shelf filing is particularly effective with color coding because a quick visual check can reveal any major filing errors.

The disadvantages are that units must be emptied to be moved and may need to be disassembled. Also, unless the files are in a secure area, there is no deterrent to an unauthorized person's taking a file. In case of fire, the records are susceptible to water damage, as well as harm from the flames.

However, you can purchase open shelf equipment with doors that recess into the units. Then the cabinets can be closed and locked. Rotary open shelf units have files on either side. The units rotate so that half the files are available at any one time. These units can also be closed at night by rotating the shelves so that one end of the shelf faces outward.

Compactable files (also called movable or high-density files) are a variation of open shelf filing that conserves additional space. The open shelf files are mounted on tracks imbedded in the floor. The filing units slide along the tracks so users can get to the records they need. Aisle space is conserved, but all records are not available at the same time.

Compactable files do require building alterations (i.e., installing the tracks). Therefore, moving the units is expensive and usually requires vendor assistance. Also, because the file units themselves are heavy and consolidate a great many records in a very small space, reinforcing the floor may be necessary.

Compactable systems come in three basic types. The first is a totally manual system where the user grasps a handle and slides the shelving units along the track. Mechanical-assist systems use a chain and sprocket mechanism, similar to that in a bicycle, to make moving the units easier. There are also totally automated versions where all the user has to do is press a button and the files open at the desired point. The length of the shelving rows, the height of the units, and the weight of the materials to be stored on the shelves determine which type of system is most appropriate.

Compactable files are an extremely space efficient equipment option for central file rooms. The units can and should be closed up at night and locked. Closing the unit protects the records from water damage in case of a fire. The records are also better protected from fire damage if the unit is closed.

Motorized Files

Motorized files bring the record to the user instead of the user's going to the records. The files are stored on shelves in a large, enclosed metal unit that looks like a huge box. The operator stands or sits before the unit and presses a button to indicate the appropriate shelf. The shelf is then automatically moved into position in front of the operator for retrieval.

Motorized files do provide fast access with a minimum of operator effort. And the units store large amounts of records in a small amount of space. However, only one person can use a unit at a time.

Moreover, the units are extremely expensive to purchase, as well as costly to install and maintain. The files must be installed by a vendor, and moving the units is quite costly. A service contract is needed, and if the company is not located in a major metropolitan area, repairs can be a problem. While the files can usually be hand cranked if there is a breakdown, this process is very slow and cumbersome.

Since motorized files are extremely heavy, floor reinforcement is usually needed. An additional drawback is that partially filled units must be loaded in such a way that filing weight is evenly distributed throughout the unit.

As you've probably guessed, I don't advocate these units for most filing situations. (Smaller motorized units specifically designed for storing card files, microfilm, microfiche, and aperture cards can be useful.) The money spent on the motorized files could be better spent converting the paper records to another medium. The files are an expensive short-term solution.

Color Coding Your Files

Color coding is an inexpensive way to enhance your filing system. Color coding speeds the retrieval and refiling of records while reducing misfiles. As an added benefit, it can brighten the entire office environment when used in an open shelf filing system.

With numeric filing systems, a different color is used for each digit from 0 to 9. This system creates bands of colors in the files and makes it easy to spot a misplaced folder. Thus, in a terminal digit system, if 1 is red and 7 blue, all files with numbers ending in 17 form a red and blue band. Usually all digits in the number are not color coded because a too heavy use of color lessens the impact and makes spotting errors more difficult. As a general rule, don't color more than four digits.

With alphabetic systems, a different color is assigned to each letter. Usually the first two letters of the last name are color coded. Color-coded year labels are also available. These ensure that a 1995 file doesn't accidentally get placed in the 1994 section. The year labels also make it easy to purge all files created in a certain year.

A wide range of color-coded systems are available from suppliers. While most systems are designed for the side tab file folders used in shelf filing, some color-coding supplies are available for top tab folders used in file drawers. Today systems are even available that allow you to design and print your own colored file labels in house.

Colored file folders are useful to differentiate files that might otherwise be confused. For example, one training and consulting firm uses blue folders for its client files and green folders for files on the speakers they use. However, since colored folders cost more than their manila counterparts, be sure you have a good reason for using them. Also always be sure that the label contains all necessary file information because color-blind individuals may not be able to identify the folders by color.

However you elect to use color in your files, keep the system(s) simple and easy to remember. Use distinctive colors that stand out clearly. And remember, color does not eliminate the need for a logical filing system, but it does support and enhance the system.

"Out" Cards

Out cards are another filing system aid. Not only do the cards identify who has the records, but they also speed refiling since the files person can go directly to the out card.

Out cards come in two basic varieties. The first is the card-stock version where you write directly on the card who took what file. The second version (and the one I prefer) is the vinyl type with two pockets. The smaller pocket holds a charge-out slip, while the larger pocket is used to hold any documents that may have come in for the file while it was checked out. If you use a two-part charge-out form, the copy goes in a tickler file under the date when you'll follow up if the file has not been returned.

The major difficulty with out cards is getting people to use them. In a central file room, this isn't a problem. Filing personnel realize that the cards make their lives easier, and they use them. But if users are accessing the files directly, they're almost always in "too much of a hurry" to complete a card. One approach you might try is to assign a different color card to each individual. I've had some success with this system as it appeals to the user's ego—"these are *my* cards and no one else can use them."

Bar Coding Files

If you've established a central file room and users are allowed to check files out, you may want to automate checkouts through bar coding. The principle is virtually identical to that used in library charge-out systems. The folders are bar coded. When a user checks out a file, the file bar code and the user's bar code are scanned into the system. When the file is returned, it's rescanned.

Such systems provide a fast, easy way to monitor file activity. Most commercial records management software packages have bar coding modules available. (Note: Even with bar coding, I recommend inserting a blank out card in the space where the record was removed. Refiling will be much faster.)

Other Filing Aids

If you have a problem with file folder labels peeling off, you can buy clear Mylar covers to place over the labels. The covers are inexpensive and really work.

To reduce filing errors, any time you start new filers, have them place a colored card, such as an out card, behind each item that's filed. After they file for an hour or so, check their work. If the filing is correct, they can stop using the cards. This may seem unnecessary, but I've seen plenty of situations where individuals either did not understand the filing system or did not care about the quality of their work. One person filing inaccurately for one day can create problems that could take years to correct.

"The Floating File"

One file management problem faced by virtually every file room is the "floating file." In this scenario, the person checking out the file passes it on to another individual without notifying the file room. The second individual passes it on to a third, and so on. When the records staff tries to locate the file, the person who checked it out responds, "I gave it to so-and-so a week and a half ago." The records staff then begins tracking the elusive file.

The only way to avoid the problem completely is to not check out files. If that's impractical, the following actions will help. First, establish a policy that the person checking out the file is responsible for it until he or she either returns it or notifies you that it has been passed on. Second, shorten the time period for following up on checked out records. Files won't travel as far. A third possibility is to attach routing forms to each file. Then if the file is transferred, the person transferring it can simply remove one of the routing forms, write on it who took the file, and send the form to central files.

Paper—Here to Stay

While document imaging is an increasingly large part of the records management scene as I'll show in the following chapter, the records manager is making a grave mistake if he or she ignores paper files. While paper is not glamorous or "sexy," it is still the predominant records medium and will continue in that role for some time to come. The key to success is identifying the best medium for each record category and then designing an effective system using that medium.

11

Document Imaging

Document imaging is the generic name for any technology that captures the image of a paper document and stores it on another medium. If the document is stored on computer-readable media, the process is referred to as electronic document imaging (EDI). However, you shouldn't ignore the predecessor to electronic imaging: micrographics.

While electronic imaging hasn't eliminated microfilm's usefulness, it certainly has reduced the need for it. To put matters simply, micrographics is a good technology for documents that must be retained for long periods and that are infrequently referenced. Electronic imaging is better for documents that are retrieved frequently or that are part of work-flow applications.

This chapter covers the pros and cons of both technologies, as well as explains how to perform a needs analysis to determine the system or systems best for your organization.

Micrographics

I'll begin by defining a few terms. "Microfilm" is a fine-grain high-resolution film that can record images greatly reduced in size. Microfilm may be either roll film or microfiche. "Microfiche" are sheets of film (approximately 4 inches by 6 inches) containing a number of images in a grid format. "Microforms" are another name for the various film formats. "Micrographics" refers to the technology of recording images on microfilm.

Advantages and Limitations of Microfilm

When we think of the advantages of microfilm, space savings immediately springs to mind. Microfilmed records typically save up to 95 percent of the space occupied when the records are kept on paper. A roll of microfilm typically holds more than 2,000 images. Depending on the format, a microfiche may hold from 60 to more than 200 images. This space savings results in a reduction in filing equipment. (However, electronic imaging can provide even greater space savings.)

Records protection is another advantage. As discussed in Chapter 9, duplicate sets of film can be stored off-site for a minimal cost. File integrity is preserved because documents are filmed in a fixed unalterable sequence. And, if certain conditions are met, microfilm is generally admissible as evidence in a court of law.

Microfilm is also the most durable storage medium. If properly processed and stored, silver gelatin ("wet silver") microfilm has a life expectancy of 500 years. Even more important, microfilm is a mature technology and not vendor proprietary, so you don't have to worry if a supplier goes out of business. Readers to view the film and reader-printers to make copies of the film are basically generic pieces of equipment that will always be available.

Although microfilm has many advantages, there are also some definite limitations. One is the need for a reader to view the film. Since a reader does not replace a computer terminal, the user may need two pieces of equipment in the work area.

The physical condition of the document will have a direct impact on film quality, and both size and physical condition can affect the ability to use an automatic document feed to expedite filming.

Microfilm does not work well with current frequently updated files as you cannot keep adding documents to a roll. Thus an active file might be spread over several rolls of film, making retrieval slower than for a paper file. In addition, there is a time lag between when documents are filmed and when the film is ready for use.

Microfilm "jackets" (a form of microfiche) do allow new documents to be added to the same fiche. However, the process is quite labor intensive and cumbersome, especially when compared to electronic document imaging.

Last, but not least, the issue of user resistance to film must be considered. Microfilm is not as "user friendly" as electronic imaging. While electronic imaging can have a retrieval time of a few seconds, searching a computer index to determine the document's film location, manually retrieving the film cartridge, and inserting the film in a reader may take a few minutes.

Uses of Microfilm

Electronic imaging has greatly reduced the use of microfilm. I now primarily recommend microfilm for documents that must be stored for eight or more years and that will be referenced infrequently. For example, employee medical records must be retained for thirty years after termination. Microfilming these files after the employee terminates saves money and space. I prefer film for these records as the odds of retrieval are very low. If they are electronically imaged, they will need to be transferred to later generations of disks periodically. Otherwise, you won't be able to find equipment to read them.

Other Considerations

Microfilming is a highly technical process. Given its gradually decreasing use, I now don't recommend purchasing equipment to film documents in-house unless the organization already has a filming operation in place. In most locations, you should have no difficulty finding a reputable service bureau to do your filming and processing.

Even though you may not be filming in-house, there are some technical considerations of which you should be aware. First, to ensure its longevity, the film must be properly processed and stored. A reputable service bureau will process your film in accordance with ANSI (American National Standards Institute) standards.

The original film should be stored off-site in a climate-controlled facility. Users should work with a duplicate copy. Storing the original off-site ensures that you have backup protection if the copy is accidentally injured or destroyed. It's preferable to store the original off-site instead of a copy because some quality is lost with each "generation" of film—just as a photocopy of a photocopy will not be as sharp as a photocopy of the original. By protecting the original, you'll always be able to work from a first-generation copy.

While the ANSI standards for film storage vary with the type of film, the two basic issues are temperature and humidity. For long-term or archival storage, the maximum temperature should not exceed 21°C (70°F). While different types of film can tolerate different levels of relative humidity, the 30 to 40% range is satisfactory for all types.

Film stored off-site should be checked periodically in accordance with the appropriate ANSI standard to ensure that no deterioration has occurred. (See the Bibliography for a listing of major micrographics standards.)

Readers

While using a service bureau eliminates the need for cameras, you will need readers and reader-printers to reference the film. In selecting readers, a key consideration is how heavily they will be used. If a reader will be used for extended periods of time, investing in a top quality unit is important. For heavy use, "blowback" of 100 percent or more is desirable. In other words, the image appears as large as or larger than the original document. However, for infrequent viewing of originals with fairly large type, a blowback of 75 percent might be adequate.

Other features that are important if the unit is to be used heavily are adjustable screen angles, matte or dull finish screens, and tinted screens.

Other considerations are the sharpness of the screen image, the illumination, and the focus. The screen image should be uniformly sharp and readable over the entire screen area. The illumination should be comfortable for sustained reading without being either too bright or too dim. And the illumination should be fairly even over the entire screen. The reader should be easy to focus, and you shouldn't need to refocus frequently when moving from image to image.

The reader should also be sturdily constructed with a heavy large base to ensure that it won't be tipped over easily. Maintenance, such as changing bulbs, should be easy to do. And if the unit is a portable, it should be able to withstand drops, bumps, or other "hard knocks."

In addition to projecting an image on a screen, reader-printers also make hard copies of the image. Since you are really buying a photocopier as well as a viewer, it's important to determine how many copies you'll be making. Like photocopiers, different models are geared to handle different levels of copying. Today virtually all reader-printers make plain-paper copies.

If your film is computer indexed, you will probably want a reader that interfaces with your computer system. With a CAR (computer assisted retrieval) system, when you insert the appropriate roll of film in the reader, the reader automatically advances the film to the desired image.

Legality of Microfilm

As already noted, microforms are generally accepted by both state and federal government as copies admissible as evidence in courts of law. The primary basis is statutory, under the Uniform Photographic Copies of Business and Public Records as Evidence Act (UPA) and the Uniform Rules of Evidence (URE). States that have not adopted one or both of these pieces of legislation have adopted similar statutes addressing the legality of microfilm.

In addition, most government and regulatory agencies have established policies and statutes accepting microfilmed records. However, some agencies, such as the Internal Revenue Service, do have specific requirements that filmed records must meet to be accepted. Donald S. Skupsky's *Recordkeeping Requirements* (see Bibliography) has an extensive discussion of the statutes governing the legal acceptance of microfilm.

Electronic Document Imaging

Electronic document imaging is the newest star on the records management horizon. With such systems, documents are scanned and digitized. The digitized images may be stored on a hard drive, optical disk, or other computer-readable media. The documents are computer indexed and may either be viewed on a terminal or printed in hard copy form by a laser printer.

Storage Media

When considering imaging from a records management view-point, the media the documents are stored on becomes an important issue. While document images can be stored on a hard drive, such images can be altered or deleted. If the documents you are imaging are of legal significance and you wish to destroy the paper, then the images need to be stored on a more permanent medium.

The two "permanent" storage media are CD-ROM and WORM (write once read many times) optical disks. Rewritable optical disks are also available, but, as with a computer hard drive, images can be replaced. With both WORM and CD-ROM systems, once the documents are written to a disk they cannot be removed or altered.

But there are some important differences between the two media. With a WORM system, documents can be added to the disk over an extended period of time until the disk is filled. However, with CD-ROM all documents are written to the disk at once (or possibly in a couple of sessions). If a file is being added to steadily over a period of months or years (such as a personnel file), the file will be spread over many CDs. This will slow retrieval time and may pose problems when files are past their retention. Also, in a small system, documents may have to be accumulated for a period of time until enough material is collected to fill a disk.

On the other hand, WORM systems are vendor proprietary while CD-ROM is a fairly generic technology with industry standards. CDs also are much less costly than WORM disks and are easier to duplicate. "Jukeboxes" are available for both types of disks. These devices automate the retrieval of a specific disk and enable many disks to be readily accessible. However, retrieval of documents from CD-ROM is slower than from WORM disks.

CD-ROM is most effective for storing reports and other documents where there will be no subsequent additions to the file. WORM, on the other hand, is ideal for files that remain active for extended periods and are added to regularly.

One problem in writing about technology is the rapidity of change. It is only recently that low cost CD recorders became available, thus making it possible for an organization to economically produce its own CD-ROMs in-house. It is certainly conceivable that in the future, documents can easily be added to CD-ROM disks, much as they are now added to WORM disks.

Advantage of an Electronic Imaging System

Whichever medium or combinations of media you choose, imaging provides a number of benefits to the user. These include:

Highly compact storage. Depending on size and type, the disks may hold anywhere from a few thousand to several hundred thousand pages. The reason I'm not being more specific is that any specific figures would be obsolete by the time of publication. Enormous progress has been made in this area. Disks that once held 60,000 pages now hold 200,000!

Integration of document management, data management, and text processing. Most systems permit data to be input by a variety of means: scanning of hard copy or microfilm, keyboard entry, and transfer from the computer system. The user can review both document images and computer data simultaneously through "windows" on the terminal screen.

Computer indexing of data. Depending on the software used, documents can be indexed and retrieved by a wide range of fields. If the documents are text scanned as well as image scanned, they can be searched for any term or combination of terms in the document. Indexing is an area I'll return to since it is critical to the system's success.

Rapid retrieval. Users can retrieve documents at their terminals without going to a file room or pulling rolls of film and inserting them in a reader. The actual retrieval speed will depend on such factors as the number of users, the number of disk drives, the size of the disks, whether the desired disk is already in the drive, and so on. However, retrieval time when the disk is in a drive will be a few seconds.

Concurrent access to data by multiple users. With a networked system, multiple users can review the same document simultaneously. This eliminates problems with "checked out" records and allows users in different offices to discuss the same record over the phone.

Improvements in document flow and transmittal. Documents can be routed electronically from one individual to another. This, of course, is considerably faster than transmitting paper and eliminates the risk of the document's being lost. Thus, insurance claims or credit card applications can be processed electronically within the organization.

Ease of updating files. Files can be added to indefinitely. However, since retrieval speed is faster if all of the documents in a file are on the same side of the same disk, instead of filling up one side completely, you may want to spread files over several disk sides. Thus, personnel records for employees A–D might be on disk A, side 1, E–H on disk B, side 2, I–M on disk B, side 3, and so on, even though you could have fit A–M on one disk side. This way as new material comes in, it can be written to the appropriate disk, thus speeding retrieval of the complete file.

Be sure, however, that the system you select has this capability because not all systems do. Also, as discussed earlier, such grouping of documents is not possible with CD-ROM at this time.

Disks that do not need special environmental protection. Because the disks are hermetically sealed, you do not have to store them in a climate-controlled facility. The longevity of disks is increasing steadily. At this time, many vendors are guaranteeing twenty- to thirty-year lives for their disks. However, a bigger issue than disk longevity is the ability to obtain equipment to read the disks. As the technology improves, images will have to be moved to later versions of the storage medium if you are to continue to access them.

Other Considerations

As you can see, optical disk technology offers a number of exciting benefits. However, other factors that must be considered are:

System cost. While you can set up a low-end imaging installation for less than $10,000, especially if you take advantage of equipment already in place such as a PC and a laser printer, large networked systems represent a major capital investment that can run into millions of dollars. Cost-benefit analysis is discussed later in this chapter.

Lack of industry standardization. While the situation has improved somewhat in this area, lack of standardization is still an issue. CD-ROM technology is somewhat standardized, but WORM systems are not. Much of the technology and software is still vendor proprietary, although now multiple suppliers make equipment that can be used with the major systems. And most imaging systems are now compatible with Windows.

There's currently a great deal of debate about whether or not the lack of standards is a problem. After all, companies typically commit to a primary vendor for their main computer systems, and no one expects to be able to load a DEC disk in an IBM drive and read it. There has been some movement toward standardization in the 5 ¼-inch optical disks, and it's conceivable that eventually we may have the same type of compatibility that exists for personal computers may be developed in the smaller optical disk systems. CD-ROM is leading in that direction.

Legal acceptability of document images. The situation has definitely improved in this area since I wrote the second edition of this book. There is still no general statutory basis for the legal acceptability of optical images unless you interpret the statutes governing microfilm as applying to imaged documents. Some experts do interpret them in that light, but others do not.

However, some federal agencies are now accepting imaged information and allowing the companies using imaging to dispose of the paperwork after the documents are imaged, but other federal agencies still require the retention of paper. Some states have passed statutes providing for the legal acceptability of imaged records. I have not listed specific states or agencies because statutes are changing constantly. Undoubtedly more regulations will have passed before this book is published.

So whether or not you can dispose of documents after they are imaged depends on your organization's location and the agencies that regulate its activities. Consult your legal department in this area, and act in accordance with its advice.

One final word of advice—if the decision is to dispose of the original documents (and many organizations are doing just that), document all imaging system procedures. Should your imaged documents ever be called into court, your system will have more credibility if all operating procedures and quality control checks are clearly spelled out and you can demonstrate compliance with them.

System life span. One reason some organizations have rejected imaging technology is a concern about the ability to access records in future years. While microfilm readers are relatively generic and will continue to be available, with imaging you are committed to a specific system. Therefore, key considerations are whether equipment to support that system will continue to be available and whether you'll have the funding to move older records to more current technology.

One issue here is the life of the records. Records being kept for six or fewer years probably won't have to be moved to a later generation of disks. But longer lived records probably will.

A second factor is supplier stability. If the supplier has installed a large number of systems, equipment undoubtedly will continue to be available or conversions will be possible. But if you purchase from a supplier with only a few installations and the firm subsequently goes out of business, you might have serious problems.

System Components

An imaging system requires a number of components. These include the following:

• Scanners. The first step in converting a document to disk is scanning it. Scanners come in a wide range of models from table-top units for scanning letter- and legal-size documents, to large units for scanning engineering drawings. There are also microfilm scanners. Most scanners have automatic document feeds, and some units can scan both sides of a page simultaneously.

The two most important issues with scanners are scanning resolution and speed. "Scanning resolution" refers to the number of dots or pixels per inch at which the material is scanned. Higher resolutions improve image quality, but they increase the amount of space the document requires on the disk, hence lowering disk capacity and slowing scanning speed.

Scanning at 200 pixels per inch produces legible copies of office records in good condition, while 300 pixels per inch produces material equivalent to laser printer output. At 400 pixels per inch, the copy will closely resemble the original.

Speed will depend on the scanner's capabilities, the scanning resolution, and the amount of material on the document. For example, it will take much longer to scan a single-spaced form with small type than it will to scan a double-spaced half-page long memo. Document quality is also a factor, affecting whether the documents move smoothly through the automatic feed or there are frequent jams.

Hence, you can't simply rely on the vendor's estimate of the number of pages per minute. You'll need to test the equipment thoroughly with the kinds of documents you'll be inputing to get an accurate estimate of the system's speed.

- User Workstations. If users do not already have high-resolution monitors, their systems may need to be upgraded so they can view documents clearly. Individuals working extensively with the system may need 19-inch monitors so they can take full advantage of windowing capabilities.

- Software. The key to the entire system is software. Imaging software ranges in a price from around one hundred dollars to hundreds of thousands of dollars. Some software is primarily designed for document retrieval, while other packages are geared to expedite work flow. First of all, determine what the system should be able accomplish. Then identify those packages that can meet your objectives. Also consider your users' needs and level of familiarity with the system. Infrequent users need a very "user-friendly" system.

- Servers and the Network. The server supports the entire system and controls its operation. Documents are held in one or more servers until they are written to the disk. Likewise, when documents are retrieved, they pass through the servers. Having an adequate number of servers is essential if retrieval speed is to meet user expectations.

Images occupy far more space on a computer system than data files. Hence, it is essential that the network have the size and capabilities to support the imaging system. While two minutes spent retrieving an imaged file is far faster than the time spent pulling a paper file, two minutes spent looking at a blank computer screen is the longest two minutes in the world.

▪ The Disks. While CD-ROM disks are fairly standardized, WORM disks come in many types. At this time, the vast majority of systems use either 5¼-inch or 12-inch disks. Key issues are the number of records you need to maintain on-line and retrieval speed. It is faster for the system to search the smaller disk. On the other hand, less data can be available on-line with the smaller disks because they hold less and the jukeboxes that contain them hold fewer disks.

▪ Disk Drives and Jukeboxes. Small systems may only have one disk drive. With such systems, an operator loads the appropriate disk into the drive to search for a document. Larger systems use either autochangers or jukeboxes that automatically load the appropriate disk into a drive when a document is requested. Units come in all sizes from a three-disk autochanger to jukeboxes holding hundreds of disks. Jukeboxes may have one or multiple drives. The more drives, the faster the retrieval speed.

▪ Laser Printers. When a hard copy of a document is needed, it is generated on a laser printer. Issues here are the speed of the printer, the resolution or sharpness of its output, and the size or sizes of paper it will accommodate. Again, it is important to test output quality on your documents. One organization discovered after purchasing a system that while notes in the margins appeared on the workstation screen, the printer "clipped" them off because it didn't print all the way out to the edge of the paper.

System Design Considerations

When you talk with organizations that have optical disk systems in place, you hear reactions ranging from great satisfaction to complete dissatisfaction. When you talk further with these companies, a pattern emerges. The organizations that are happy with their systems did their homework carefully. Often a year or more is spent assessing the situation, gathering data, and preparing the request for proposal. The ones that are unhappy didn't research the situation carefully. They thought they could throw hardware at their records problems and have the problems go away.

Using a Team Approach

Imaging has become an increasingly complex process. While systems can be extremely successful, they can also be colossal failures. To avoid problems, it is essential that there be a broad-based approach to implementing the technology.

First of all, departments should get approval from a centralized group or task force before implementing imaging applications. This is even more of an issue now that imaging can be installed for less than $10,000. Many departments are buying inexpensive imaging systems without doing their homework. Then they often discover the system does not meet their needs and discontinue using it. Even if the system is adequate, it can be incompatible with other systems within the organization, and therefore information cannot be easily networked.

Successful imaging applications require a team approach. Since imaging represents a major change to computer operations, the systems staff must be involved in the process. As records manager, you should also be a team member. Since records are being created, all of the records management considerations apply, including:

- Records retention
- Records backup and vital records protection
- Legal considerations, including whether the originals need be retained
- Long-term perspective; not just how the system will work now, but how it will work when it's fully loaded
- Indexing of information for easy retrieval
- Physical issues connected with document conversion

Many of the system problems I've learned about occurred because the records management issues just listed were not considered. For example, at one seminar, I had two individuals from the human resources department of a major corporation announce that they had installed an optical disk system for benefit and pension records. They stated their major goal was to eliminate hard copies of these records. When I inquired if their legal counsel had approved the destruction of the originals after scanning, I learned that they had not even been aware that destroying the originals might pose a legal problem.

Of course, system users also need to be heavily involved in the process. The user group should include individuals who will work with the system every day as well as managers and supervisors. Again I have seen problems arise because no one consulted those individuals who were most familiar with the records and who would actually be inputing information on the system.

Performing a Needs Analysis

The first step in the needs analysis is identifying the applications that might benefit from imaging. Rank these applications in order of priority for imaging. Since one system may not meet all your needs equally well, you want to be certain that the highest priority needs are satisfied. Also, while many different types of records may benefit from imaging, you should implement applications gradually. Be sure one application is running smoothly before you add another.

For each potential imaging application, consider the following factors:

The physical characteristics of the records to be scanned. For example, what are the originals—engineering drawings, checks, 8 ½-by-11-inch single sheets, or bound books? You'll need to consider their size, the weight and color of the paper, and whether both sides have to be scanned. All of these factors will affect your choice of equipment.

Also, don't forget the overall quality of the documents. Are they faded third carbons or clean originals? If the paper is brittle or very fragile, it won't be able to pass through an automatic document feed. To ensure that the equipment you select can handle your records to your satisfaction, prepare a test package of examples of the poorest quality materials that you expect to scan.

Have each supplier scan the materials in your presence. (Don't leave the materials with the vendor since you want to see what image quality is under normal circumstances.) This type of test will prevent unpleasant surprises after you've purchased the equipment.

Another factor to consider is possible forms redesign. Printing forms on a heavier stock can reduce paper jams. And since graphics consume considerably more disk space than typed text, you may want to keep to a minimum the amount of artwork used on forms.

The volume of the records created, retrieved, and filed. Measure carefully, and be sure to take into account any seasonal variations. This information is essential for determining the size of the system.

Consider both the initial scope of the system and how it will need to grow. If you will eventually need a large system, be sure that the system you select can be expanded to meet your future needs. For example, if you will need a jukebox in the future, be sure the system can be upgraded to accommodate one. And don't depend on supplier promises to expand the system in the future. These often do not materialize. Verify that larger systems are already in place at other organizations and working successfully.

The records' retention period. It's senseless to convert records that are near the end of their retention period to another medium. Likewise, if the records have a short retention period and are referenced infrequently, imaging may not be cost-effective.

Microfilming is often done to conserve space for records with long retention periods. While you'll have to calculate the relative costs for your organization, a rough rule of thumb is that it's usually worthwhile to film if the records will be kept at least eight years. Also, if the records are vital, filming duplicate copies for off-site storage is cheaper than making and storing duplicate paper copies.

Your primary benefits with electronic imaging are greater productivity and more efficient document retrieval. Electronic imaging is rarely if ever justified solely from the point of saving space and storage costs, especially since the records may need to be moved to later generations of the technology.

Identifying the system's primary objective. Is your goal to improve the retrieval and storage of documents or to simplify work flow and document transmission? Work-flow applications are considerably more complex than storage and retrieval applications.

If the system is work-flow oriented, you'll need to chart the flow of relevant documents through the organization. What changes in that flow do you want? This is an excellent time to re-engineer processes and bring about changes.

Disk clustering and disk retention. As discussed earlier, you'll probably want to allocate disk space so that, if possible, all the documents in a particular file will be located on the same disk. And since documents cannot be removed from a WORM or CD-ROM disk, all of the documents will have the same retention period. This, too, may affect how you group materials on the disks.

The retention issue can be addressed another way. You can periodically copy active files to a new disk. Inactive files can be copied to an "archive" disk to be stored for the remainder of their retention period. Or, if the inactive documents are past their retention, they would not be recopied and the old disk would be destroyed. Of course, if the documents are stored on a hard drive or rewritable disk, they can simply be deleted when their retention is past.

Conversion of old files. Converting older files tends to be extremely costly and labor intensive. If files do need to be converted because they are still active, you'll need to decide whether to do the conversion in-house or hire a service bureau. Keep in mind that scanning and indexing documents are skilled tasks. As many companies have learned the hard way, you can't simply bring in temporaries with no training and expect satisfactory results.

Most organizations are only doing limited conversions of old documents. If the files are still active—such as personnel files for active employees—they are converted. Inactive files are not converted.

System backup and archiving. Although disks are not vulnerable to temperature or humidity changes, they certainly can be destroyed in a fire or other disaster. Therefore, duplicate copies of the records should be retained off-site. With WORM systems, most organizations are using magnetic tape as the off-site backup medium since copying the disks is cumbersome. However, if you are using CD-ROM as your storage medium, making an additional set of duplicate disks is a simple, low cost alternative.

Ability to interface with existing systems. Whenever possible, you'll want to take advantage of technology that is already in place. Hopefully, at least some of your equipment needs can be met by hardware already in place. If you have existing computer indexes or an existing microfilm system, you will probably want to merge these into the new system.

Microfilm can be scanned and digitized. Whether you will be satisfied with the quality of the end product depends to a large extent on the quality of the original film. All of the major microfilm equipment suppliers do offer reader-printers with the capability to scan and digitize film. While you can then transfer the images to computer-readable media, if the retrieval needs are minimal you are probably better off maintaining the documents on film.

The vendor's financial stability and prior experience. Far more suppliers are offering imaging products or services now than will be in a few years. The market simply isn't there to support all of the existing firms. Therefore, you want to be sure that the supplier or suppliers you choose have staying power. Several suppliers have already gone out of business, leaving users in awkward positions. Others have remained in business but discontinued their involvement in the imaging industry. And even if someone "buys out" the supplier, the rules of the game may change. One company, whose vendor was bought out, found out that the new owners of the company refused to honor the warranty if the equipment were moved to a new location!

Have your finance department carefully evaluate the financial stability of the company. Don't assume that because a company is large, it is stable. And for privately held companies, insist on audited financial statements. Other safeguards including making sure that there are at least two manufacturers of every system component and having software coding and documentation placed in escrow. Then if the firm does not survive, your staff can at least access the coding and documentation.

You'll probably also want a supplier with considerable experience, although some companies opt to be "beta sites" or experimental locations. There are often substantial cost incentives for being a guinea pig, but there is also substantial risk. Such ventures tend to be most successful if you have a strong in-house systems staff who are willing to be actively involved in the project.

With suppliers, you now have a choice between companies that sell you a system with their name on it and system integrators who compile a system for you using components from multiple suppliers. Yet another option is having your own systems staff function as an integrator. This latter approach assumes very strong, motivated in-house systems support.

There are pros and cons to each approach. A good idea is to consider all possibilities. Get proposals from companies who sell complete systems as well as from system integrators. Decide which approach best meets your needs.

Indexing the records. The key to prompt retrieval is effective indexing of the imaged documents. As discussed in Chapter 10, the two basic indexing options are (1) inputing critical information into a computer database that can then be searched and (2) OCR indexing of the text. Before making a final decision as to which approach to use, test both options carefully with heavy involvement from users who will actually be retrieving documents.

Database indexing requires careful definition of the fields. Since it is estimated that one in 350 key strokes contains an error, you do want to minimize actual data entry whenever possible. Whenever choices are limited, pop-down menus listing the possible entries can reduce the amount of key strokes. OCR indexing is an option if you are working with clean, neatly typed documents and if the terms you wish to index by are contained in the document. And, of course, it is possible to do both types of indexing.

Another approach to indexing that can be combined with either or both of the methods just discussed is bar coding documents. With this system, some indexing information is communicated through a bar code that is either printed on the document or affixed by a label. The bar code is scanned at the same time as the rest of the document. One possible application is bar coding purchase-order or invoice numbers so that they can automatically be entered into the system and matched with other accounting data already on the network. Another example would be bar coding hospital patient records with the patient's number. Then all documents pertaining to that patient would automatically be indexed accordingly. One big advantage of bar coding is a very low error rate—approximately one in three million items entered.

The Cost-Benefit Analysis

In spite of the high cost of a large optical disk system, many companies who have installed such systems feel that they have been financially justified. Others have installed systems because functioning with paper or microfilm was no longer viable. For some, more rapid customer service was the deciding factor.

However, even if monetary factors are not the only basis for the decision, they will be a major consideration. To perform the cost-benefit analysis, you'll need to compare the cost of the imaging system with the cost of your current paper- or film-based operation. Normally, I only project the data out for five years, because by the end of that period, you're sure to be making major changes or enhancements to the system.

To determine the cost of your present operation, consider:

1. The cost of the space occupied by the active records. Don't forget to include aisle space as well as the actual square footage occupied by the filing cabinets. Typically, each file cabinet requires between 6 and 10 square feet.
2. The cost of storing the inactive records. If you are storing records in-house and don't have accurate cost data, assume approximately $5.00 per box per year.
3. The cost of the time spent processing, handling, and filing the records under the present system. Also consider the time spent searching for misfiles. An imaging system should virtually eliminate this problem.
4. The cost of additional filing equipment and supplies.
5. Photocopying costs. An imaging system should dramatically reduce the need for photocopies because multiple users can reference documents simultaneously on the computer system.

In addition to the cost of all the equipment required for the optical disk system you select, you'll need to consider both startup costs and operating costs. Startup costs include:

- System installation costs
- Training of personnel

- Conversion of old documents (if appropriate)
- Modification of existing forms and procedures to accommodate the new system

Operating costs include:

- Equipment maintenance contracts
- Annual software licensing fees
- Cost of disks (don't forget backup media)
- Space occupied by the equipment
- Time spent scanning, indexing, retrieving, and printing documents
- Paper and printer supplies for those situations when hard copies must be created
- If documents are not being destroyed after they are written to, you'll also need to consider the cost of storing them off-site.

COLD (Computer Output Laser Disk)

I have primarily been discussing source document imaging. However, computer data can also be written to either CD-ROM or optical disk. This technology is known as COLD, and it is rapidly replacing its predecessor COM (computer output microfiche). In the past, computer reports were often printed on microfiche. While this process provided faster retrieval and lower costs than generating the same reports on paper, COLD now provides far greater space savings and retrieval speed than COM.

An organization can either generate the disks in-house or it can send its tapes to a service bureau that will prepare the disks, indexed according to agreed upon specifications, and return them to the company.

To Image or Not to Image?

The decision whether to implement an imaging system is a complex one. Obviously, imaging systems can greatly expedite document retrieval and use. They also enable an organization to protect large active files from destruction in a disaster. However, successfully implementing an imaging system requires considerable time and effort on the part of many individuals. The most common mistake I see in this area is inadequate preliminary analysis. Someone decides imaging will be advantageous. A very limited number of systems are evaluated, and one is purchased. After the purchase, it's discovered that the system does not meet the real needs of the organization.

Don't rush into this decision! You'll be living with the results for many years. Buying a system quickly because "there's money in the budget this year" is a major mistake. A failed system can cause major credibility problems and make it very difficult to ever get another system in the door.

Each organization must make the decision based on its own needs and requirements. And, of course, one possible decision is to do nothing at this time. Some companies are waiting until electronic document imaging is a more mature technology before taking the plunge. However, keep in mind that no computer-based technology ever really stabilizes. Systems are continually improving. At some point, you need to "jump in."

Even more so than with micrographics, implementing an electronic imaging system is a complex and highly technical process. Also the technology is advancing daily. I've tried in this chapter to provide a thorough overview of such systems while trying to avoid statements that would be out of date before the book was published. The Bibliography does list additional resources. Also, as with micrographics, the Association for Information and Image Management (AIIM) is an excellent resource for current information (see the Appendix).

12

Forms and Reports Management: Controlling Records From Creation

When preparing this edition, I debated including forms and reports management. While I firmly believe these areas are important aspects of information management that should be addressed on an organization-wide basis, I am also a realist. At this time, many organizations either have no forms and/or reports management function or, if they do, the responsibility rests somewhere other than with records management.

I finally decided to discuss these areas because I believe strongly that records managers should be involved in these functions, even if they do not have overall accountability for them. I also feel that those organizations who ignore these areas are losing productivity and wasting money. Unnecessary or badly designed forms and reports waste the time of everyone involved with them. So, this chapter addresses both areas, taking into account the impact of computers and office automation on each.

Forms Management in the 90s

Computers have changed many forms. We now have the "paperless" form—designed, completed, stored, and transmitted electronically. Many paper forms are now machine readable, thus making processing them much easier. However, the overall use of forms has not diminished, a fact taxpayers are painfully aware of every spring.

Forms management involves analyzing the user's needs to determine what form (if any) is needed, designing the best possible form to meet those needs, and ensuring that the form is efficiently produced and available to the user. The overall objectives of the process are to increase organizational efficiency and productivity while reducing costs.

Forms management achieves these objectives through the following actions:

- Eliminating unnecessary forms, unnecessary copies of forms, and unnecessary items on forms
- Consolidating forms that serve similar purposes
- Preventing unnecessary new forms and unnecessary revisions to existing forms
- Designing forms for maximum effectiveness
- Determining the most appropriate medium for each form and ensuring its availability to users

Even if forms management is not part of your responsibilities, you should have a working knowledge of this area for two reasons. First, as you've probably already noticed, records management uses quite a few forms. Second, the company's forms can have a major impact on your job, especially in the area of document imaging. If forms are printed on very thin paper, you may have difficulty scanning or filming them. Whether or not the paper is colored and which copy of a multipart form you receive will affect filming or scanning. Hence, it's in your best interest to coordinate efforts closely with the company's forms designer if the responsibility is not under your jurisdiction.

Numbering

Forms are, of course, records, and as we've discussed, it's important to easily identify records. The forms number is the unique identifier. Many organizations have a standard forms numbering system already in place. However, if such a system doesn't exist, establishing one is simple.

The most effective systems tend to be the simplest. You're not trying to capsulize all relevant information about the form in the number, but simply to provide a unique identifier for that form. Consecutive numbering is the easiest system. You assign each form a four digit number, beginning with 0001. Since forms are revised frequently, add A for the first printed version (1099-A, for example). When the form is revised, you go to 1099-B, and so on. Or instead of an alpha code, you can use the revision date, as in 1099-6/90. However, using a revision date makes the number longer. Also, users may feel that a perfectly good form is "out of date" because its date is not that current.

Very large organizations may preface the form number with an alpha code to indicate the form's use or function, such as HR001-A for forms pertaining to human resources. Avoid linking forms numbers to specific organizational units such as departments or divisions. If there is a reorganization, the whole system may become invalid.

I do recommend assigning numbers to electronic forms. If desired, the form number can be coded to indicate that it references a computer created and stored form.

Analysis and Design

Forms analysis and design are two major ongoing activities in any forms management program. Analysis identifies the user's needs that must be met by the form, while design uses the information collected from analysis to develop the best possible format. Normally one individual—a forms analyst—performs both the analysis and design functions for a particular group of forms.

Analysis

The analyst needs answers to the following questions regarding the form's content, usage, and physical features.

Content

1. What information does the user need to collect on the form? Note the emphasis on "need." The user should be able to justify every item he or she wants on the form. It's also a good idea to have the user indicate which information is most important.

2. Can any of the questions on the form have multiple-choice answers? Listing the various answers speeds completion of the form. Also, multiple choice options can be machine readable, making for faster, more accurate data compilation. Of course, you can always use "Other: _____" for situations that aren't covered by the given categories.

Usage

1. Who will be completing the form? What's their educational background and level of familiarity with the material on the form? If, for example, customers will complete the form at home, you need to provide very comprehensive, simple instructions.

If everyone completing the form works for your organization, you may want to maintain the form electronically instead of as a paper form.

2. How many copies of the form will be used in a year? Normally you don't want to spend a great deal of time designing a low-usage form (fewer than 500 copies a year)—it simply isn't cost-effective. For low-usage forms only used within one department, you may want to have the department design the form and possibly even print copies as needed from the computer. Some organizations do not even worry about incorporating such forms in their forms management program.

3. Where will the form be completed? The conditions under which the form must be completed may affect its physical design. For example, a shop supervisor may need a "book" of maintenance forms that can be stuck in a pocket, while a clerk at a desk can work well with an 8½-by-11-inch form.

4. Who needs copies of the form? You want to keep the number of copies to a minimum, as extra copies have a habit of creeping into files and records storage. Also they add cost.

5. Does the form relate to other forms, either as a source of information for them or as a result of them? If it does, get samples of the other forms and explore the possibility of consolidation. Even if you can't consolidate the forms, you do want to design them as a system so that they complement each other.

6. Is the form a source document for computer input? If so, it must be developed so that data can be transferred easily. If pos-

sible, develop a form that can be scanned rather than requiring manual data entry.

Physical Features

1. Will the form be scanned or microfilmed? Scanning or filming the original or first copy improves image quality. And, as discussed earlier, the weight and color of the paper may make a difference.

2. Does the form have any special size requirements? How will it be filed? For example, must it fit in a card file or binder?

3. How long will the form be kept? Any new document you create should have a retention period assigned. If you do not have the forms management responsibility, make sure you are notified whenever a new form is created so that a retention period can be assigned. With a centralized forms management responsibility, it's easy to become part of the process. With a decentralized approach to forms management, you'll have to identify new forms each year when the retention schedule is revised.

Design

Once the analyst has collected all of the preceding information, he or she is ready to prepare a rough draft of the form. The first step is sorting all of the desired information into logical groups, such as customer name, address, and phone number. Next, these groups should be arranged in a logical order—logical, that is, for the completer and the processor of the form.

Finally, the rough draft is prepared. This draft should be photocopied and copies given to the user for testing. Testing is the most important step in the whole process and should be done for every new or extensively revised form. Even if the user tells you the form looks perfect, test it. Only testing in real-world situations will indicate if the form really works. Too many firms have learned this lesson the hard way by printing forms and then discovering problems using them that necessitated starting over.

Forms design is not a difficult or complicated art—not, that is, if you follow these rules. They will help you create forms that are efficient, economical, and attractive.

1. *Use the box or ULC (upper-left caption) design.* As shown in Exhibit 12-1, this design enables you to fit more items into less space, speeds completion if the form will be typed or filled in on a computer by reducing the amount of spacing and tabbing, and reduces the chance of misplaced information.

Whenever possible, line up the caption boxes as shown in the ULC example in Exhibit 12-1 with the employee number, home telephone, and zip code. This reduces the number of tab stops needed and is visually more appealing.

2. *Use clear, descriptive captions.* Words like "name," "number," and "date" may mean one thing to you and another thing to the person completing the form. For example, on an insurance form, "date" might mean either when the form was completed or when the accident occurred.

3. *Leave ample space for writing information.* If the forms are to be completed on a computer or typewriter, align the lines to match the equipment's spacing. For horizontal lines, allow 2 inches for the first ten characters and 1 inch for every seven to eight additional characters. If you don't know how long a name will be, allow at least 3 inches. And if the data will be entered in a computer, use "tick marks," not boxes, to indicate the number of spaces in the data field. (Boxes make it difficult to transfer data accurately.)

Acceptable:

Unacceptable:

If you want people to write comments on the form, draw lines for them to write on. The lines motivate the users to write more than a large blank space does. They also help control extremely large or small handwriting and make it easier to read.

4. *Always put the form number in the same place.* There are four schools of thought as to the preferred spot: upper-left corner, lower-left, upper-right, lower-right. It really doesn't matter which you choose as long as you're consistent.

5. *Allow at least a ⅜-inch margin all around the form* and a ¾-inch margin on the left-hand side if the form is to be three-hole punched. The margin serves several purposes. First, printing presses do not normally print to the edges, and extending the lines

Exhibit 12-1. Acceptable and Unacceptable Caption Designs

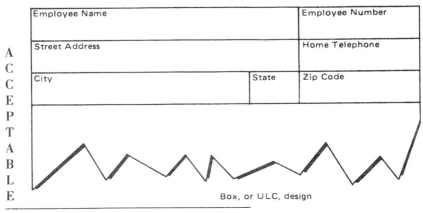

A
C
C
E
P
T
A
B
L
E

Employee Name		Employee Number
Street Address		Home Telephone
City	State	Zip Code

Box, or ULC, design

U
N
A
C
C
E
P
T
A
B
L
E

Employee Name _____

Street Address _____

City _____ State _____ Zip Code _____

Employee Number _____ Home Telephone _____

Unacceptable design
(uses more space; slows down completion if form is to
be completed on a computer or typewriter.)

Employee Name   Employee Number

Street Address   Home Telephone

City   State   Zip Code

Unacceptable design
(unclear as to where information should be written)

through "bleeding" is expensive. Second, margins increase the form's readability. Also, if the form will be scanned, you won't run the risk of losing information because the scanner doesn't read to the edge of the page.

6. *Use a sans serif typeface for captions, headings, and short instructions.* Use serif type for lengthy instructions or text. Serifs are the angled lines, or "feet," extending from letters. This book is set in a serif typeface. Helvetica and Univers are commonly used sans serif types, while Century is a popular serif type. Serif type is easier to read in text because the serifs break the monotony, but sans serif is "cleaner" and more effective for headings, captions, and other short items.

7. *Write clear, concise instructions.* If several steps are involved, number and list them. For example:

To report a theft:

1. Complete sections 1, 2, 3, and 5 of this form.
2. Send the white and yellow copies of this form to your insurance agent, along with a copy of the police report.
3. Keep the green copy for your records.

Ideally, the form should be self-explanatory so users don't have to refer to a procedures manual to find out how to complete it. If the instructions are too long or too complex to fit on the form itself, you might print them on a thin cover sheet that can be torn off and referred to while the form is completed. If the forms are contained in a "book," another option is printing the instructions on the inside cover. Never print the instructions on the back of the form. Most people overlook them, and in any case, it's very frustrating to keep having to flip the form over to read them.

8. *If a form is multipart, indicate the proper distribution order,* either in the instructions or at the bottom of the form. Using different colors for each copy also helps ensure accurate distribution. If you will be scanning or microfilming the form, design it so that a white copy will be scanned or filmed.

9. *Use chemical carbonless paper for multicopy forms.* This paper is sometimes incorrectly referred to as NCR (no carbon required) paper, but in reality NCR is the trademark for Appleton Paper's

brand of chemical carbonless paper. One big advantage of such paper is that you can usually print the forms in-house, while carbon-interleaved or snap-out forms must usually be done by an outside printer. Forms printed on chemical carbonless paper take less storage space, are cheaper to ship, and are generally preferred by users because they are less "messy." However, in a few cases, you may need carbon sets because they can produce more copies.

The Printing Decision

An increasing number of forms are being generated in-house. The decision as to whether to print in-house or go outside should be based on the in-house print shop's ability to do the work in terms of both equipment and time, as well as the comparative cost. Low-usage forms may be printed from computer files or photocopied on an "as-needed" basis.

One option you may want to consider is having an outside firm provide a complete forms management program. A number of vendors provide such programs. These programs are tailored to your company's individual needs, but typically they include:

- Designing all forms
- Warehousing the forms
- Providing a complete inventory control service
- Delivering forms to the client as needed

Depending on your in-house capabilities and your forms volume, you may find such a program to be cost-effective. The major advantage is that it provides you with a complete, professional forms management program that requires much less effort on your part than staffing an in-house function. The major drawback is that you become totally dependent on an outside supplier. If problems develop, it can be difficult and time-consuming to extricate yourself from the relationship. So if you are considering such a program, choose your supplier carefully.

Order Quantities and Reorder Points

Major benefits to maintaining forms on-line are that they can be revised as needed, are never out of stock, and are always current.

However, for high-volume paper forms, a critical issue is determining how much to order and setting the proper reorder point. Never order more than one year's supply of any form at a time because it may need to be revised unexpectedly. Even if you feel you have the "perfect form," circumstances beyond your control may make it obsolete. For example, the phone company might change the area code for your region, or your company might be acquired by another and be renamed.

If a form is very heavily used, you may wish to order less than a one year's supply to minimize storage costs or allow you the flexibility to modify it during the year.

After you've decided how many forms to order, you need to set an appropriate reorder point. Then when the supply room notifies you that point is reached, you have ample time to get a new shipment in without the form's being out of stock. The factors you'll need to consider in setting a reorder point are:

- The time needed for users to approve a reprint or request changes
- The time needed to implement any changes and place the order.
- The time needed to print the form on a normal, not rush basis, to avoid overtime charges
- Amount of safety stock—a one month's supply of the old forms on hand when the new ones are delivered
- Any seasonal variations in usage

In most cases, you'll probably find setting the reorder point at a three months' supply will work well. But for heavily used or very important forms, it's a good idea to calculate the reorder point on a case-by-case basis using the above criteria.

Eliminating Obsolete Forms

Ideally, users should notify you when a form becomes obsolete. However, if you wait for that to happen, you'll soon have a supply room full of obsolete forms.

Consequently, you need to take the initiative. A good policy is to check with the users on all forms that have not been ordered for two years to see if they are still in use. When a form is discontinued, destroy any leftover blank copies and do not reuse the form number.

The Need for Reports Management

While forms are perhaps the most obvious cause of excess paperwork, another formidable contender has entered the arena—namely, the report. With the advent of data processing, we have acquired the capability to classify, arrange, and present large masses of information in virtually an infinite number of combinations.

And we have done just that until the average manager is inundated with reports—some of great importance, others "not worth the paper they're written on." The report has also become a corporate status symbol for some insecure managers. They feel they need to be on every distribution list to demonstrate their importance in the corporate hierarchy.

As a result, in many organizations, the report has moved from being a useful information tool to becoming a major problem area. Reports management reverses that trend by controlling the production of reports and insuring that they provide the maximum benefit to the organization.

What Kinds of Reports?

Since we've identified computer-generated reports as the major cause of the reports explosion, it might seem logical to assume that reports management should deal exclusively with these reports. However, the scope of the program should be broadened to also include all manually generated reports that are sent between departments on a regular basis. Why? Because although they are fewer in number, manually generated reports can also waste a great deal of time and money.

Here's a classic example. At one company, the president decided to send the board of directors a monthly report on the company's progress. Sounds like a good idea, doesn't it? Well, in a little over a year, the report grew from 15 pages to more than 100. It became a competition between the eight vice presidents who submitted data to see who could produce the longest section and include the most graphs. The legal department would take four pages just to explain that there had been no changes in the cases in litigation. Producing the report tied up the corporate communications staff for more than a week each month and reduced the print shop to chaos because there were always last minute changes.

And what did the recipients think? When one board member was asked for his opinion, he said, "I have my own business to run. I don't have time to read all this." A much better alternative would have been a concise two- or three-page summary of key events in the past month. But as so often happens, the recipients' needs were forgotten by the producers of the report.

When you're evaluating the manual reports, don't worry about one-time or intradepartmental reports, such as a comparative analysis of some new software or an employee's monthly progress report to his or her boss. These reports are best left to the discretion of the individual manager. Your concern is with the reports that consume significant amounts of time and money.

Objectives

Just as with forms management, the two primary goals of reports management are to improve efficiency and save money. These goals are achieved through the following processes:

- *Eliminating unnecessary reports.* Many reports are unnecessary because users can access the needed information directly from the computer system. Others are produced long after the need for them has ended. The initial reports management effort must "clean house" to eliminate all such reports regardless of the storage medium. Thereafter, all reports must be regularly reevaluated and their continued existence justified.

- *Consolidating reports whenever possible.* Are several departments receiving similar, but not identical, reports? If so, investigate consolidating them. Demonstrating to the departments the cost savings of the consolidation will help motivate them to work with you.

▪ *Redesigning the contents of reports to increase their effectiveness.* Such redesign can include eliminating unnecessary data and adding useful information such as summary data. It can also mean rearranging items on the report so they'll be easier for the user to work with.

One caution, though, with some computer-generated reports: Compare the cost of making the change with the benefits it provides. Sometimes a change that seems simple may be costly to implement because of the way the initial programming was done or because that programming was never properly documented.

▪ *Limiting distribution of reports when appropriate.* Everyone who receives a report should need it as part of his or her job. If the need isn't there, the report shouldn't be either. Actually, many people appreciate this aspect of reports management. They are afraid to say that they don't need a report for fear it will appear that they're not doing their jobs as thoroughly as they might be.

Some managers have no real need for the report but will say, "I need to check it occasionally." Others may feel that they lose status if they don't have access to the report. If the report is on a COLD (computer output laser disk) system, users can reference it as needed. Another alternative is to keep copies of the reports on file at the company library or information center. Then if these managers do want to see the report occasionally, they can. Such a center also allows managers to reduce their in-office active storage of copies of these reports.

▪ *Limiting the number of copies produced.* There's a tendency on the part of many managers to order excessive numbers of copies of reports. For example, the manager might decide, "We'll need five copies—one each for Kathy, Joe, Mandy, and Francine, and one for the files." However, if the users don't need to see the report immediately after it is run or won't be working extensively from it, copies can be routed or shared. In our example, Kathy and Joe might share one copy, which is then filed, while Mandy and Francine share a second copy. We've now eliminated three copies.

▪ *Reducing the frequency of reports when appropriate.* Some reports are produced more often than necessary. At one company, sales reports were produced daily, weekly, and monthly, but the users only worked with the weekly and monthly versions. Hence,

A Commercial Records Center With a Bar-Coder Locator System.

Photo Courtesy of Commercial Archives.

Lateral Filing Equipment.

Photo Courtesy of TAB Products Co.

Open-Shelf Filing Equipment.

Photo Courtesy of TAB Products Co.

Rotary Files Use a "Lazy Susan" Concept to save Space.

Photo Courtesy of TAB Products Co.

Bar Coding Expedites Checking Out and returning Files.

Photo Courtesy of TAB Products Co.

Electronic Compactable Files.

Photo Courtesy of Spacesaver Corporation.

Work Flow Software Adds Value to Electronic Document Imaging.

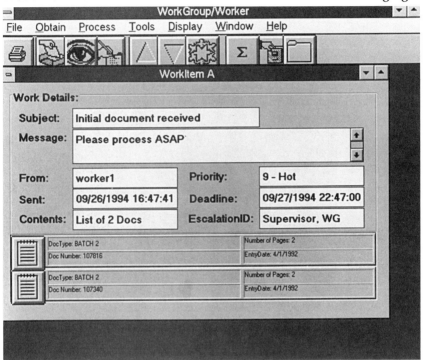

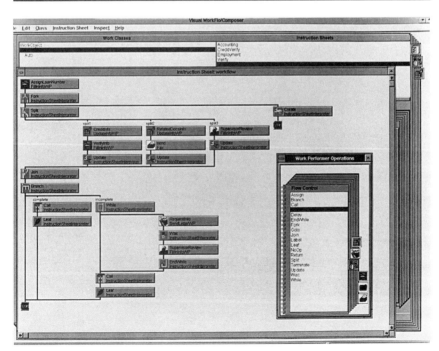

Photos Courtesy of Filenet Corporation.

Two Optical Disk Storage and Retrieval Units (Jukeboxes).

Photo Courtesy of Filenet Corporation.

eliminating the daily report was a logical step. Also some users didn't need the weekly report. Another easy change was sending them the monthly copy only. Instances like these are not uncommon. There's a tendency to base a report's frequency on how often we are capable of preparing it instead of how often we need it.

- *Using COLD when appropriate.* As already discussed, reports can be stored on CD-ROM or WORM disks, saving both space and money while improving retrieval speed. However, be sure the information is needed before converting it to COLD.

- *Eliminating the report altogether* by storing data on-line and letting users reference it on their terminals and print only the portions they need printed.

Selling the Reports Management Concept

Selling reports management to the company's upper management group is relatively easy because of the program's cost-effectiveness. Most organizations don't know what they're spending on reports. Once they become aware of that cost and once they realize reports management can usually save a minimum of 10 percent of that figure and probably much more, they become quite receptive to the idea.

Also, senior management usually gets the heaviest barrage of reports. These individuals know they have problems coping with the influx of data, and they tend to welcome help.

Just as with records management in general, you can sell the reports management program more easily if you find and document one or two "horror stories." Look for some high-cost reports that are overdistributed and poorly designed. Then show how these reports could be improved and the resulting cost savings. Explain that you want to apply that same concept on a larger scale, concentrating on those reports that cost the most to produce.

While most middle managers will be receptive to the program, a few may fear that you're "taking over" their reports and trying to limit the information they receive. You'll need to stress that your goal is making information more accessible and more economical. If departments are "charged back" for the reports they receive, they'll be more receptive to the concept. It will also help if your department has already gained credibility and trust through the successful implementation of other aspects of records management.

Where to Begin

A reports management program begins with an inventory. Collecting this data will be simplified because most of the reports will be generated by one department—the data processing or systems group.

For a reports management program to be successful, the records management group must work closely with the systems staff. In fact, in some companies, reports management is a systems department responsibility. However, this often means that manually prepared reports are excluded from the program. Hence, it's usually best if the program is a team effort.

The systems staff should be able to provide you with the following data for each report they run:

> Report number
> Title
> Department(s) requesting the report
> Frequency of distribution
> Distribution list
> Cost of producing and distributing the report

Either you or the systems staff will then need to contact the department or departments requesting the report to determine its purpose. A form similar to Exhibit 12-2 can be used to collect this data.

The same types of information will need to be collected for manually prepared reports. The one area that will differ from computer-generated reports is cost. With manual reports, you'll need the hours of employee time spent preparing the report. These hours can then be converted to dollars by using standard hourly rates for each job category. You can obtain these rates from the human resources department; do make sure they include an allowance for fringe benefits.

Exhibit 12-2. Sample Reports Inventory Form

REPORTS INVENTORY			
Report Title			Report Number
Dept. Requesting or Originating Report			

Purpose of Report:_____

	Distribution (indicate if more than one copy sent)		
Frequency ☐ daily ☐ semianually ☐ weekly ☐ annually ☐ monthly ☐ other ____	Name	Department	No. of Copies
Cost (use average figures)			
Data processing costs ____ Printing/Photocopying ____ Mailing ____ Graphics ____ Word processing ____ Other ____ ____			
Total ____ ____			
Time (do *not* include EDP time computed above) Hrs. managerial ____ Hrs. secretarial ____ Hrs. clerical ____ Hrs. other ____			
Completed by		Dept.	Date

Ranking the Reports

After you've collected the survey data, the next step is to rank the reports according to cost of producing them. Ranking is important because you'll want to concentrate your primary efforts on the most costly reports. It's not practical to spend ten to twenty hours redesigning a report that costs a few hundred dollars a year to produce. For these reports, you may want to simply determine whether or not it is necessary to continue producing it. On the other hand, if the report costs several thousand dollars a year, the time spent redesigning it is easy to justify.

Contacting the Recipients

The next step is contacting the users of the reports. For senior management, you'll probably want to schedule interviews and discuss all the reports they receive in one session. For other users, simply send them a questionnaire similar to Exhibit 12-3. Explain in your cover letter that if you don't receive a reply by a certain date (usually two or three weeks later), you'll assume that they no longer need the report and drop them from the distribution list.

The questions on the form are fairly self-explanatory. If recipients indicate that they just "review" the report and don't take action based on it, sharing a routed copy or having access to a "library copy" will probably meet their needs. Many people will welcome the opportunity to shed painlessly the reports they don't need.

Taking Action

After you've received all of the responses from users, you can begin taking appropriate action. If no one needs the report, eliminate it. If someone doesn't need the report, drop them from the distribution list. In short, look for the quick fixes—actions that can be taken easily and that will result in immediate benefits. After you've completed these quick fixes, document the cost savings and report to management on the program's progress to date.

Then address the changes in the reports' contents and design. For multiuser reports, you may need to schedule some meetings

Exhibit 12-3. Sample Report Recipient Questionnaire

REPORT RECIPIENT QUESTIONNAIRE

To be completed by report recipient or interviewer

Report Title		Report No.
Recipient	Department	Phone

1. Do *you* still need the report?   ☐ Yes   ☐ No

    a. If "yes," explain briefly how you use the report.

    _____

    _____

    b. If "no," don't complete remainder of form.

2. Do *you* need to receive the report as frequently as you do now?

    ☐ Yes   ☐ No

    If "no," how frequently do you need to see the report?

    ☐ daily   ☐ monthly   ☐ annually

    ☐ weekly   ☐ semiannually   ☐ other _____

3. How can this report be improved?   _____

    _____

    _____

    _____

    _____

    _____

    _____

Prepared by	Date

to make sure everyone's needs are met. Again, after the changes are implemented, document the cost savings and productivity improvements and report to management.

An Ongoing Program

To avoid repeating this process, make reports management an ongoing program. A key aspect of this program is the policy that all computer-generated and interdepartmental manual reports that are prepared repeatedly must be approved by the reports management function. Also, every two years, you need to reevaluate any report that has not been changed or reviewed in that period. This review is accomplished by sending each recipient a questionnaire similar to Exhibit 12-3. And, just as before, your cover letter should explain that recipients will be removed from the distribution list if they don't reply in a timely manner.

Another technique you can use for eliminating unnecessary reports is the "see if anyone notices it's gone" strategy. You simply don't send out the report and see who calls to complain. Those who don't call are removed from the distribution list. While this technique has worked successfully for many organizations, be sure you have appropriate management support before using it. And don't try it with any reports that are clearly vital to the organization's operations and well-being.

All in all, reports management is one of the easiest aspects of records management to promote because it is cost-effective and because top management sees its benefits directly as the number of reports it has to cope with diminishes.

13

Documenting the Records Management Program

Up to now I've covered how to develop an effective records management system and supporting procedures. However, having a well-designed system is not enough. You must also communicate the system both to its users and to those who will help you implement it. The records manual is your communications vehicle. It also is a critical part of the ISO quality certification process.

Yet documentation is the biggest problem for most organizations seeking ISO 9000 certification. While these organizations are making quality products or producing quality service, they have not documented the steps they follow or how they ensure proper recordkeeping. Manuals have become a joke instead of a valuable resource at many organizations. All too often the manuals become glorified dustcatchers that are never opened by the users. One reason manuals are ignored is that the users are often ignored when the manual is written.

Identifying the Manual's Users

To ensure that your manual is a useful tool, begin by identifying the potential users. Typically, they fall into two major categories.

The first group is the records coordinators and any other individuals who will be involved in implementing the program. These individuals need two types of information: (1) an overall understanding of the program and their responsibilities within it, and (2) the practical information necessary to implement the program on an ongoing basis.

The second group is the staff of the records management department. In addition to the information needed by the records coordinators, they must also have detailed procedures for the internal operations of the records management program. For example, these might include how to assign box numbers to records going into storage and how to enter the appropriate information in the index database.

One caution: Don't forget to write the staff procedures. I've often heard it said: "We're a small department, and we know what we're doing. Why waste time writing it down?" Well, small departments are the most vulnerable. I could cite several instances where the only person who knew how to do the procedure was taken ill or left abruptly, causing major problems.

Now the obvious question is how to meet the needs of all of these special interests without either overwhelming everyone with a monster manual that documents all the program's details or writing two separate manuals. The answer is to develop a "core" manual and build upon it.

The records coordinators and other key users receive the core manual that contains the overall policies and the general procedures and other information they need to comply with the program. The records management staff receives internal procedures, as well as the external ones. You may want to print the internal staff procedures on colored paper to differentiate them clearly from the core manual.

Issuing the Manual in Sections

As already discussed, developing a comprehensive records management program takes time. Consequently, it is appropriate that the manual be developed in conjunction with the program, instead of after the entire program is operational.

If you follow this approach, the section order of the records manual will depend on how your program has evolved. For example, if your program began with records retention, the first three sections of the manual to be issued would be:

- Records Management Policy
- Records Retention

- Records Center

Records Management Policy

This first section should state the organization's overall philosophy of records management and the responsibilities of key personnel. The overall policy statement might be:

> XYZ Company's policy is to maintain a companywide records management program to manage the creation, use, storage, protection, and disposition of the company's records in an efficient, economical manner. The records management program includes:
>
> 1. Establishing and managing retention periods for all company records, retaining them only as long as needed for administrative, legal, fiscal, or historical purposes.
> 2. Transferring records to storage when they become inactive but must still be retained.
> 3. Using appropriate technologies such as document imaging to enhance records retrieval and use and to conserve space.
> 4. Protecting vital records from destruction or loss.
> 5. Assisting individual departments in the development of effective records management systems for their active records.

The key personnel whose responsibilities would be given include the records manager, any supervisors reporting to the records manager, the department heads, and the departmental records coordinators. With the exception of the department heads, the statements of responsibility can be condensed from the job descriptions for the various positions.

The department heads' responsibilities are:

1. To ensure that the records management program is fully implemented in their areas, in compliance with corporate policies and procedures.

2. To appoint records coordinators for their areas.
3. To ensure that these coordinators have the time and resources needed to perform their job.

Spelling all this out may seem like you're belaboring an obvious point. But it is essential that department heads realize that the records management policy is just as important as any other corporate policy they must comply with.

This section of the manual is usually the same for both versions. It might also include a "whom to contact" page that tells a user whom to call if he or she has questions about a particular aspect of the program. If you include this information, try to use job titles, not names, as the information will be less likely to be outdated. If you do use names, be sure to issue revisions whenever new individuals take over the various positions.

If you have an overall corporate policy manual, you may want to include the records management policy in this manual as well. Don't, however, try to incorporate the entire records manual into a general corporate manual. Buried in such a work, it will be overlooked. Also revisions will need to be coordinated through the individual responsible for the corporate manual, thus making updating your material a much more cumbersome process than it need be.

Records Retention

This section of the manual should include information on how to use the retention schedule; the procedure for requesting additions, deletions, or changes to the schedule; and the schedule itself. Exhibit 13-1 includes typical information on using the schedule and requesting additions, deletions, or changes. In the records management staff version, you will probably want to include the procedure for updating the schedule annually.

Records Center

The core version of this section should state the center's purpose (storage of inactive records in accordance with the official retention policy). It should also give the procedures for transferring

(text continues on page 186)

Exhibit 13-1. Sample Text From Records Retention Section of the Manual

---

How to Use the Retention Schedule

The records retention schedule lists the categories of company records maintained by different departments. The listing includes records stored on paper, microfilm, and computer-readable media. The schedule does not list computer printouts retained for less than one year (many daily and weekly reports). Departments are expected to dispose of these reports as quickly as possible and in no case to retain them for longer than one year.

The record categories are grouped first by department number and then listed alphabetically by title. Unless otherwise indicated, the retention periods are given in years.

How to Request a Change to the Retention Schedule

To add, delete, or change a retention schedule entry, make a copy of the form on the following page and complete it. Have your department manager and division head sign the form. Then submit it to the records manager.

Requests to redistribute the total retention period between office and storage locations only require the records manager's approval. Example: changing a retention from 2 years in the office and 5 years in storage to 3 years in the office and 4 years in storage.

Requests to add or delete record categories or to change total retention periods must be approved by the records manager, the general counsel, and the tax director.

REQUEST FOR RECORDS RETENTION SCHEDULE CHANGES

Name: _____ Phone Ext.: _____

Department Name: _____ Date: _____

_____ Please add the following records to our department's retention schedule:

Record Title   *Medium*   *Office Retention*   *Storage*

_____ Please delete the following records from our department's retention schedule:

Record Title   *Reason for Deletion*

_____ Please make the following changes to our department's retention schedule:

Current Entry:

Change to:

Reason for Change:

Department Manager's Signature	Date
Division Head's Signature	Date

For Records Management Staff Use:

Records Manager's Signature	Date
General Counsel's Signature	Date
Tax Director's Signature	Date

records to the center, requesting records from the center, and destroying records at the end of their retention procedures.

The contents of this section will depend heavily on whether you use a commercial records center or operate your own facility. If you operate your own center, you'll need extensive internal staff procedures on such areas as indexing records, assigning box numbers, retrieval of records, follow-up on checked out records, and so on. If you use a commercial facility, the staff procedures will be much briefer and will coordinate with the vendor's internal procedures. You may even be able to use or adapt the standardized procedures that many commercial centers give to their customers.

Other Sections of the Manual

As you expand the program, other sections will be added to the manual. Typically, these would include:

- Vital Records
- Filing Systems
- Document Imaging
- Forms and Reports Management

Vital Records

Here you have a choice. You can incorporate the vital records material in the records manual, or you can include it in the disaster recovery manual (assuming one exists) and simply reference this manual in the records manual.

Whichever alternative you elect, this section should include:

- The company's official definition of a vital record
- The procedure for determining if a record is vital, including a discussion of the vital records committee's role in the process
- The procedure for duplicating records and sending them off-site to the vital records center
- The vital records schedule
- The procedure for retrieving records if necessary

General users and coordinators need to know what records are vital and what their responsibilities are in terms of ensuring that these records are protected. The records management staff procedures should detail the day-to-day operations of the program.

Filing Systems

This section's contents depend on the type of controls you have in place for filing active records. If there is a central files program, it should include procedures for sending records to central files, retrieving them, and returning them. These procedures would appear in both versions of the manual. The manual for the records management staff should also include the procedures for the internal operation of the central files room.

If there is a uniform filing system, the manual should contain the various classifications in the system, their definitions, and an index to the system. If the uniform system is used on a decentralized basis instead of in a central files room, the core manual should explain how to implement the system on a departmental basis.

On the other hand, if each department maintains its own files without the benefit of a uniform filing system, this section might simply note some general filing guidelines and tips.

If files audits will be conducted, this section of the core manual should state the procedures that will be followed, the standards that must be met, and the follow-up for departments not in compliance. The core manual should also state the company's policy on purchasing filing equipment. A key part of this policy is the requirement that the records manager approve all requests for new equipment and that requests will be approved only if the department is in compliance with the retention schedule.

Document Imaging

Whether imaging is micrographics, electronic imaging, or both, the internal operational procedures should be extremely detailed and may even become a separate manual. The general user, on the other hand, needs to know how to retrieve and use records on the imaging system, as well as how to request that records be converted to a non-paper medium.

Forms and Reports Management

This information should be included only if the records manager has the responsibility for either or both of these functions. While these would be two separate sections, the contents of each will be very similar. The core manual section should begin with an official policy statement that forms (or reports) can be created only with the knowledge and authorization of the records management staff. The manual should also define forms and reports and include the procedures for:

- Requesting new forms or reports
- Requesting changes in existing forms and reports
- Discontinuing existing forms and reports

In addition to this material, the records management staff's manual should include all the internal working procedures in both areas, such as assigning form numbers and reordering forms. Typically, there will be fewer internal procedures for reports management as most of these procedures will fall under the jurisdiction of the systems department.

Preparing the Manual

Whatever topics you choose to include in the records manual, the preparation process remains basically the same. Preparing a records manual is simpler than preparing other types of administrative manuals for two reasons. First, you are the source of most of the data for the manual. Second, there is less text to write because the retention schedule comprises a major portion of the manual.

Writing the manual will be simpler if you think about it from the program's onset. Take a large file folder, label it "records manual," and drop in any materials that will be useful when it's time to start writing. Also, set up a subdirectory on your computer for the manual and copy into it any documents you've created that can be adapted for the manual. For example, your memo to senior management explaining what the program will accomplish is the nucleus of a policy statement. Then, when you start to draft the manual, much of the data you already need will be gathered together.

The Manual's Physical Appearance

Although you will sometimes see records manuals prepared as bound booklets, this is not advisable because updating the manual would then be virtually impossible. A three-ring binder is a more long lasting and practical approach. In terms of the binder's size, while you want to allow additional space for updates, you also want the manual to be "user friendly." Four-inch thick binders are difficult to handle and visually intimidating, so I suggest a 2½-inch maximum. If the manual won't fit in this size binder (which is highly unlikely), then use two volumes.

Make sure the manual's title is on the binder's spine so that it can be clearly identified. Avoid binders with pockets on the inside covers; users have a regrettable tendency to "file" updates to the manual in these pockets.

To reduce lost manuals, I place a self-adhesive label on the inside cover of each copy. Here's a sample:

Copy 15
Assigned to:
Human Resources Department
Records Coordinator

Assigning the manual to the department's coordinator instead of to an individual by name helps ensure that the manual remains in the department if the person is transferred or reassigned.

For easy referencing, each section of the manual should be identified with an index tab. The tabs should be Mylar-reinforced and should state both the section number and title ("2 Records Retention," for example). The holes on the tab sheets should also be Mylar-reinforced.

Each page of the manual should have a standard page heading that clearly identifies it as part of the records manual. Then if a page is removed from the manual, it can easily be replaced in the proper position. If your company has other manuals with standard page headings, you can model yours on those. Or you can develop a simple page design similar to Exhibit 13-2.

The subject refers to the specific topic, such as "Transferring Records to the Records Center." The number is usually a two-part reference to the section and specific topic. For example, 2-3 is the third topic in the second section. Each topic is also page numbered separately, beginning with page 1. Then if you expand 2-3 from two pages to four, the pages in 2-4, 2-5, and so on will not have to be renumbered.

Each page should also have the date that page was issued. When the page is revised, the date is changed accordingly. Then it's a simple matter for users to compare the dates and determine which page is current practice.

The Table of Contents

A records manual should have a table of contents; that is, a listing of sections and topics in the order in which they occur. The table of contents serves as the users' reference guide to the entire manual. For example, the table of contents for section 2 might read as follows:

2   RECORDS RETENTION
2–1   How to Use the Retention Schedule
2–2   Additions, Deletions, and Changes to the Schedule
2–3   General Records Categories; Duplicate Records
2–4   Records Retention Schedule

Unlike other manuals, a records manual does not normally need an index. That's because the table of contents is self-explanatory and relatively short, and because the retention and vital records schedules form their own index through listings in order of department number and then alphabetically.

Writing Clearly and Concisely

If the manual is to be a success, the text must be clear and concise. The records manual is not the place for pompous, lengthy senten-

Exhibit 13-2. Sample Page Design for Records Manual

| ⟨Logo⟩ | **RECORDS MANUAL** | Number:
Page: |
| | Subject: | Date: |

ces extolling the virtues of the records program. Two simple rules will help you avoid that problem:

- Write in the active voice
- Eliminate deadwood

Writing in the active voice means that the subject of the sentence performs the action. For example:

> List each carton separately on the records transfer list.
> ("You" is the subject and is understood.)
>
> or
>
> The central files supervisor completes the report monthly.
> ("The supervisor" is the subject.)

The active voice is concise, and it always assigns responsibility—a must in a manual. The difference becomes obvious if you rewrite the examples above in the passive voice, with the subject being acted upon.

> Each carton should be listed separately on the records transfer list.
>
> or
>
> The report is completed monthly. ("By the central files supervisor" may be added.)

The other key to good writing is eliminating deadwood, or unnecessary words. Make sure every word is there for a reason. For example, why say "in the event that" or "due to the fact that" when "if" and "because" will do the job much better? Also, avoid repetitious phrases such as "plan in advance" and "basic essentials."

Playscript Procedures

Much of the writing you'll be doing in the manual is procedural—"how to do something." Since most of these procedures involve more than one person, you'll find it helpful to write them in "playscript."* In other words, write the procedure as if it were the

---

*Playscript was developed by Leslie Matthies and is discussed in his book *The New Playscript Procedure* (Stamford, CT: Office Publications, Inc., 1977).

script for a play. The only difference is that the "actors" perform specific tasks in the procedure instead of speaking lines of dialogue. Exhibit 13-3 is an example of a playscript procedure.

As you can see, playscript forces you into a concise, logical writing style. It also makes it easy for each individual to identify his or her responsibilities. If an exception or other option occurs, it is broken out and listed separately, just as was done with 2a in Exhibit 13-3.

Do note the column proportions marked on Exhibit 13-3. Limiting the responsibility column to 2 inches is necessary if you are to have an adequate line length for the actions.

Forms in the Manual

Any forms mentioned in the manual should be reproduced in it. This enables users to know what the form looks like and ensures that they use the right form. For example, the playscript procedure just presented would include as an attachment a filled-in sample of Form 269-B. This attachment would be placed at the end of the procedure.

Producing the Manual

Of course, you'll want to prepare the manual on word processing so that it can easily be updated. While the "spell check" feature on most word processing packages is marvelous, it will not detect a typographical error in the numbers on the retention schedule. And if the correct retention is "5 years" and "3 years" is keyed in by mistake, the results could be disastrous. So proofread the numbers carefully!

Distributing the Manual

Sending the manual out in the mail with a cover letter is a virtual guarantee that it will be ignored. People are busy, and they'll put it to one side, saying, "I'll look at it when I have some free time." And, of course, they never have the time.

The best way to distribute the manual is at training sessions. During the session, you "walk" the users through the manual

Exhibit 13-3. Example of a Playscript Procedure

```
┌─────────────────────────────────────────────────────────────────┐
│                                                                   │
│  ╱◇╲                                                              │
│ ◇Logo◇   RECORDS MANUAL                    Number: 3–3            │
│  ╲◇╱                                         Page: 1              │
│  Subject:  Requesting a Record From the Records Center  Date: 8/20/x1 │
│  ───────────────────────────────────────────────────────         │
│                                                                   │
│  Responsibility          Action                                   │
│                                                                   │
│  Requester               1. Completes Records Request Form (269-B). │
│                                                                   │
│                          2. Sends completed form to records center. │
│                                                                   │
│                             a. May also call in request.          │
│                                                                   │
│  Records Center          3. Finds record's location in index.     │
│  Coordinator                                                      │
│                             a. If record is not in index, notifies │
│                                requester.                         │
│                                                                   │
│                          4. Gives blue copy of 269-B to warehouse- │
│                             person.                               │
│                                                                   │
│  Warehouseperson         5. Retrieves record from carton.         │
│                                                                   │
│                          6. Replaces record with OUT card (blue copy │
│                             of 269-B in pocket).                  │
│                                                                   │
│  Records Center          7. Attaches pink copy of 269-B to record. │
│  Coordinator                                                      │
│                          8. Sends record to requester.            │
│                                                                   │
│                          9. Files white copy of 269-B in tickler file │
│                             under date two weeks later.           │
│                                                                   │
│              2"                              4"                    │
│      [◄──────────►] [◄──────────────────────►]                    │
│                                                                   │
│                                                                   │
└─────────────────────────────────────────────────────────────────┘
```

section-by-section, highlighting key points and explaining the rationale behind the various policies. It's also a good idea to have separate training sessions for management, coordinators, and other users, because each group's needs and interests will be different.

Keeping the Manual Up To Date

Any manual quickly loses its effectiveness if it's not kept up to date. As already discussed, the retention schedule should be reviewed annually to incorporate new records and reduce retention values. You should also review the remainder of the manual annually. This review will enable you to pick up those procedural changes that were not incorporated into the manual when they occurred. The review also allows you to reassess existing policies and determine if they are still appropriate.

Don't delegate this task. You'll be surprised at the changes you'll find—even when you think the manual is up to date. However, it's a good backup to have other staff members review appropriate sections. They may catch corrections you've overlooked.

Updating the manual also involves making sure users keep their copies up to date. If you're making major revisions, have users bring their manuals to a training session. The new pages can be given out and reviewed, and everyone can update his or her manual at that time. Or if you have a limited number of coordinators, collect their manuals, replace the old material with the new, and then return the manuals. Several of my clients opt for this approach, using student work-study employees or other low-cost help to do the updating.

Another issue is getting users to note the changes in the manual. I usually print revised material in a different type style such as bold face, italics, or small caps. Then the changes can be easily spotted.

14

The Future of Records Management

This chapter explores the future of records management in two ways. The first is the program's future within your organization, while the second is the future of records management in the United States.

As already discussed, a key concern for any records manager is keeping the program alive within his or her area. The records manager must actively promote the program, keeping both users and management aware of its benefits.

Resuscitating a Comatose Program

It is easier, however, to promote and maintain a program that you developed as opposed to one developed by someone else. And many records managers are placed in the unfortunate position of inheriting a dormant program that was developed internally. This situation is actually more difficult to deal with than starting a program from scratch. With a new program, people are willing to give you the benefit of the doubt.

However, if a program has been allowed to sink into oblivion, you must begin from Day 1 to rebuild its credibility. The following is a good approach to take:

1. Identify any service problems users may be experiencing, and make every effort to correct them as quickly as possible.
2. Communicate with the users. Let them know that you've taken over the program and what changes and enhance-

ments are planned. If records coordinators have not been named, get them on your team as quickly as possible.

3. If the retention schedule has not been revised in the past two years, your first priority should be revising it.

4. Next, address the storage area. If it is not set up in an orderly manner, begin the housecleaning and indexing process.

5. If the firm's vital records are not identified and protected, begin the process of doing so, starting with the most valuable records.

6. Evaluate the departmental records systems and procedures to identify areas in need of assistance or upgrading. Usually with dormant programs, either this area has not been addressed or there is a moribund central files program. If there is a central files program, begin by improving and expanding it. If there isn't one, decide if one is appropriate and practical. If not, work with those departments with the greatest problems to establish effective active records management procedures.

7. Review any current uses of document imaging within the company, and, if appropriate, identify ways to expand the program.

8. Go the extra mile, whenever practical. If you can provide users with a little extra "hands-on" support, you'll build your credibility more quickly. However, don't promise more than you can deliver.

As part of this overall process, be sure to take time to identify why the old program was allowed to lapse. Then develop your strategy to ensure that history does not repeat itself.

Keeping Up With Changes

As you develop and strengthen your organization's program, you'll also want to keep track of where records management is going within the United States. Probably the biggest frustration for users is the complex set of legal requirements for records retention. Unfortunately, there is little hope for improvement at this time. While a number of bills to simplify retention requirements have gone before Congress, none have passed and the agencies keep churning out more legal requirements.

Also, organizations are confronted with a steadily increasing number of lawsuits. Litigation, not baseball, is the national pastime. As a result, the legal ramifications of keeping or disposing of record categories must continue to be carefully evaluated.

On the positive side, the ISO 9000 certification process is forcing organizations to place additional emphasis and resources on managing records well. Also, the technological aspect of records management keeps improving. Imaging systems are now a reality at many organizations.

The key here is making sure that you are part of the decision-making team. As discussed earlier, some organizations are making imaging decisions without input from the records management staff. In every case that I'm aware of where this was done, problems resulted that could have been easily avoided.

On the other hand, it is not realistic to assume that the entire decision on imaging systems will rest with records management. A team approach is needed with input from the systems group, the potential users, and records management, along with a careful consideration of the legal issues involved.

It is up to you to make sure that you're qualified to be part of the team. Doing your homework in terms of learning about new technological advances is a big part of the process. Another factor is keeping the users and their needs in mind.

However, as you expand your technological expertise, don't forget the basics. Having a current records retention schedule, protecting vital records, and providing users with top-notch service, regardless of the records' media, are the keys to a successful program.

Records management has always been a rewarding profession. But today's records managers have tools and resources available that were not even dreamed of ten years ago. The challenge today is blending the tried-and-true basic concepts with the technological advances to craft a program that is responsive to users' needs while protecting one of the corporation's most valuable assets—its records.

It's up to you to meet the challenge. Good luck!

Appendix
Records Management Resources

ACRC
Association of Commercial
    Records Centers
P.O. Box 20518
Raleigh, NC 27619
(919) 821-0757

AIIM
Association for Information
    and Image Management
1100 Wayne Avenue
Silver Spring, MD 20910
(301) 587-8202

ARMA International
Association of Records
    Managers and
    Administrators
4200 Somerset, Suite 215
Prairie Village, KS 66208
(913) 341-3808

Association of Contingency
    Planners
P.O. Box 341
Brigham City, UT 84302-0341
(800) 445-4ACP

BFMA
Business Forms Management
    Association
519 S.W. Third Avenue, Suite
    712
Portland, OR 97204-2519
(503) 227-3393

Institute of Certified Records
    Managers
P.O. Box 8188
Prairie Village, KS 66208

NIRMA
Nuclear Information and
    Records Management
    Association
80 Eighth Avenue, Suite 303
New York, NY 10011
(212) 683-9221

OASI
Office Automation Society
    International
5170 Meadow Wood
    Boulevard
Lynhurst, OH 44124
(216) 461-4803

Glossary

A4   The metric size of paper closest to 8 1/2″ × 11″. It is slightly longer and slightly narrower than letter size paper.

active record   A frequently used record that needs to be available for immediate access by users.

administrative value   The period of time a record may be needed within the company for administrative or operational purposes.

AIIM   Association for Information and Image Management, the professional association for the electronic document imaging and micrographics industries.

aperture card   An eighty-column keypunch card designed to hold one frame of 35-mm microfilm; primarily used for engineering drawings.

archival value   The permanent retention of a record for historical reasons.

ARMA International   Association of Records Managers and Administrators, the professional association for records managers.

ASCHII   American Standard for Computer Information Interchange, an eight-level code for data that allows 256 code combinations. It was developed to ensure compatibility between all data services.

autochanger   A device for automatically accessing optical disks and CDs.

backup copy   A duplicate of a record retained for reference in case the original is lost or destroyed.

bar code   An automatic identification technology that encodes information into an array of adjacent varying-width parallel rectangular bars and spaces.

bit   The smallest unit of information recognized by a computer.

blip   A mark on a roll of microfilm (below the image) used to count images or frames automatically.

byte   A group or sequence of adjacent bits (binary digits) that are operated upon as a unit and constitute the smallest addressable unit in a computer system.

CAR   Computer assisted retrieval; primarily used in regard to systems for computer indexing microfilm for fast retrieval.

cartridge   A container for roll microfilm that protects the film and makes it easier to load the film into a reader.

CD-ROM   An optical storage medium with a standardized format. Information is written to a CD-ROM disk in one or two sessions and cannot be deleted once it is recorded.

central files   A physical collection of files belonging to more than one individual or organizational unit.

Certified Office Automation Professional   The professional certification program for office automation specialists including records managers. It is managed by the Office Automation Society International (OASI).

Certified Records Manager   The professional certification program in records management. It is managed by the Institute of Certified Records Managers.

chronological filing   Filing in sequence according to date. Usually, the latest date is in front.

COAP   *See* Certified Office Automation Professional.

COLD   Computer output laser disk; the technology that stores computer data on CD-ROM or WORM disks for ease of retrieval by users; replaces paper printouts.

COM   Computer output microfilm or computer output microfiche; microfilm produced from on-line computer data or off-line tapes through the use of COM recorder.

commercial records center   A records center operated by a private service company and housing the records of many different companies.

compactable files   An open-shelf filing system where the shelving units are mounted on tracks and can be slid back and forth to open an aisle at the appropriate point.

critical path   The shortest time frame in which a project can be completed.

CRM   *See* Certified Records Manager.

decentralized files   Records located and maintained in or near the department immediately responsible for the function they relate to.

density   The opacity or degree of "darkness" of the background on negative film; measured by a densitometer.

diazo   One type of film used for microfilm copies. It requires ammonia for processing.

disaster recovery plan   A program of activities that should be followed in the event of a disaster. It should cover all activities, but the term is used by some organizations to indicate just the resumption of computer system operations.

document digitization   The use of scanners to convert documents to digitally coded electronic images suitable for optical disk storage.

DRAW   Direct read after write; the ability to read an optical disk image immediately after it is recorded.

duplex   A method of microfilming that captures in one exposure both the front and back of a document.

electronic mail   E-mail; the electronic transfer of correspondence and memos from one terminal to another.

facsimile   Fax; An electronic transmission of an exact duplicate of a document.

file integrity   The ability to retrieve and use a document without the chance of its being lost or misfiled.

filing inches   File volume measured in linear inches; a standard letter-size file drawer holds 25 filing inches.

fiscal/tax value   The period of time a record must be retained for financial reasons or for tax requirements.

floor load   The capacity of a floor area to support a given weight expressed in terms of weight per unit of area, such as pounds per square foot.

forms management   The function responsible for the creation, design, revision, and control of all forms within an organization.

Gannt chart   *See* Milestone chart.

gigabyte   One billion bytes.

hard copy   The paper copy of a record.

hardware   The mechanical and electronic parts of a computer; also the equipment used in a computer system.

holograph   A record in the handwriting of the person who signed it.

hypo   *See* Sodium thiosulfate.

ICR   *See* Intelligent character recognition.

inactive record   A record that does not need to be immediately available but must be retained for legal reasons or because users have an infrequent need to access it.

intelligent character recognition (ICR)   An automatic data entry system that can read hand-printed characters.

ISO   International Standards Organization; the international body that sets standards for a wide range of business and industrial activities and processes.

ISO 9000 series   A series of international standards for quality certification.

jacket   A transparent plastic carrier with sleeves to hold strips of microfilm.

jukebox   An automatic selection and retrieval device that provides rapid on-line access to multiple optical disks.

lateral file cabinet   A file cabinet wider than it is deep. Records can be arranged either front to back or sideways.

legal value   The period of time a record must be retained to meet statutory requirements or for other legal reasons.

medium   The material or substance on which information is recorded, such as paper, microfilm, magnetic disk or tape, or optical disk.

megabyte   One million bytes.

methylene blue test   A chemical test for determining the level of sodium thiosulfate remaining on film after it is processed.

microfiche   A sheet of microfilm, approximately 4" × 6", with the images arranged in a grid pattern.

microfilm   A fine-grain, high-resolution film used to record images reduced in size from the original.

microforms   The various forms of microfilm.

micrographics   The art or technology of microfilming.

middle digit filing   A numerical filing system in which the file number is divided into groups of two or three digits and is filed first by the middle group of digits, then by the first group, and finally by the last group.

milestone chart   A project planning tool that uses a vertical scale to denote the tasks in the project and a horizontal scale to indicate how long each task should take; also called a Gannt chart.

mobile aisle system   *See* Compactable files.

OCR   *See* Optical character recognition.

optical character recognition   An automatic data entry system by which printed characters are scanned and read by special equipment.

optical disk   A special disk that can store large amounts of information through encoding by a laser beam.

out card   A filing card used to replace a checked out record; usually indicates who checked out what record and when.

PERT chart *See* Project sequence diagram.

planetary camera A type of microfilm camera in which the document being photographed and the film remain in a stationary position during the exposure.

playscript A technique for writing procedures that clearly defines who is responsible for performing each action.

printout Paper output from a computer printer.

project sequence diagram A horizontal flowchart indicating the tasks in a project, their relationship, and the time required to perform each; also called a PERT (program evaluation and review technique) chart.

pulpit ladder A safety ladder having an extended top shelf; used for retrieving records stored on high shelves.

purge To remove from a file information which is of no further value.

reader A device that enlarges microfilm images for direct viewing.

reader-printer A device that enlarges microfilm images for viewing and also can produce a hard copy of the enlarged image.

record Any form of recorded information, regardless of medium.

record series A group of similar or related records, used or filed as a unit.

records center A centralized area for storing inactive records.

records center box A 15″ × 12″ × 10″ corrugated cardboard box designed to hold approximately 1 cubic foot of records, either legal or letter size.

records inventory A detailed listing of all records categories maintained by an organization; usually done as the first step in preparing a records retention schedule.

records management The systematic control of an organization's records from their creation or receipt to their ultimate preservation or destruction.

records manager The individual responsible for controlling the organization's records management program.

records retention schedule A listing of all of the organization's records categories that specifies the time period each should be retained.

reports management A system for creating, managing, and disposing of the reports used by an organization.

resolution (1) As applied to optical disk technology, the number of dots per inch or pixels that are scanned; (2) a method of measuring the sharpness or clarity of a microfilm image.

rewritable optical disks A type of optical disk that permits information to be deleted and the reuse of previously recorded disk areas.

rotary camera   A type of microfilm camera in which both the document and the film move simultaneously during the filming process.

scanner   Equipment that translates a document into digitized form.

shelf file   Side-open records storage equipment in which the records are accessed horizontally.

shredder   A machine used for the destruction of records by reducing the documents to fine strips, shreds, or particles.

sodium thiosulfate   A chemical used in processing film that removes the silver halide remaining in the film after development; also called hypo.

software   The programs that instruct a computer to perform specific functions.

source document   A record in tangible hard-copy form.

statute of limitations   A time period after an event during which a legal action or lawsuit may be initiated.

step-and-repeat camera   Microfilm camera used to produce source-document microfiche.

terminal digit filing   A numerical filing system in which the file number is divided into groups of two or three digits and is filed first by the last group of digits, then by the middle group, and finally by the first group.

tickler file   A file organized by date where documents or reminder notices are filed under the date on which they should be reviewed or acted upon.

transfer list   A list of records that are being transferred from one location to another.

uniform filing system   A standardized subject filing system used throughout an organization or a department of an organization.

vacuum drying   A method of drying water-soaked records in an airless or vacuum chamber; used to save records damaged in a disaster.

vertical file cabinet   Filing equipment that is deeper than it is wide; records are stored front to back.

vesicular film   A microfilm used for duplicate copies; processing is done by the application of heat.

vital records   Those records that are essential to resume or continue operations in the event of a disaster; to preserve the rights of the organization's owners, employees, and customers; or to protect the organization legally and financially.

vital records schedule   A listing of an organization's vital records along with an explanation of how each is to be protected from destruction in the event of a disaster.

WORM   Write once, read many times; a type of optical disk that is not erasable.

Bibliography

Alphabetic Filing Rules. Prairie Village, Kan.: ARMA International, latest edition.

Andrews, Helen N., and others. *A Report on Issues Surrounding Retention of Client Files in Law Firms.* Prairie Village, Kan.: ARMA International, 1993.

Avedon, Don. *Introduction to Electronic Imaging.* Silver Spring, Md.: AIIM, 1994.

Black, David B. *Document Capture for Document Imaging Systems.* Silver Spring, Md.: AIIM, 1992.

Bulgawicz, Susan, and Dr. Charles Nolan. *Disaster Prevention and Recovery: A Planned Approach.* Prairie Village, Kan.: ARMA International, 1988.

Cinnamon, Barry, and Richard Nees. *The Optical Disk . . . Gateway to 2000.* Silver Spring, Md.: AIIM, 1991.

Clark, Jesse L. *The Encyclopedia of Records Retention.* New York: The Records Management Group, latest edition.

Disaster Recovery Journal. St. Louis, Mo.: Systems Support, Inc., all issues will be of interest.

Document Image Automation. Westport, Conn.: Meckler Corporation, all issues will be of interest.

Eulenberg, Julia Niebuhr. *Handbook for the Recovery of Water Damaged Business Records.* Prairie Village, Kan.: ARMA International, 1986.

Federal Regulations Involving Records Retention Requirements for Businesses in Canada. Printed and distributed by Association of Records Managers and Administrators, Inc., Box 6587, Station A, Toronto, Ontario M5W 1A0.

Fire Protection for Archives and Records Centers (NFPA 232AM). Quincy, Mass.: National Fire Protection Association, latest edition.

Glossary of Records Management Terms. Prairie Village, Kan.: ARMA International, latest edition.

Guide to Record Retention Requirements in the Code of Federal Regulations. Washington, D.C.: U.S. Government Printing Office, latest edition.

Guideline for a Vital Records Program. Prairie Village, Kan.: ARMA International, latest edition.

Guideline to Job Descriptions. Prairie Village, Kan.: ARMA International, latest edition.

Guideline to Records Center Operations. Prairie Village, Kan.: ARMA International, latest edition.

How to File and Find It. Lincolnshire, Ill.: Quill Corporation, 1989.

ID Systems. Peterborough, N.H.: Helmers Publishing, Inc., all issues will be of interest.

Imaging. New York: Telecom Library, Inc., all issues will be of interest.

Imaging Product News. Potomac, Md.: Phillips Business Information, Inc., all issues will be of interest.

Imaging Technology Report. Larchmont, N.Y.: Microfilm Publishing, Inc., all issues will be of interest.

Inform. Silver Spring, Md.: AIIM, all issues will be of interest.

Information Management Sourcebook: The AIIM Buying Guide & Membership Directory. Silver Spring, Md.: AIIM, published annually.

International Micrographics Sourcebook. Larchmont, N.Y.: Microfilm Publishing, Inc., published annually.

Knutson, Joan, and Ira Bitz. *Project Management: How to Plan and Manage Successful Projects.* New York: AMACOM, 1991.

Managing Office Technology. Cleveland: Penton, all issues will be of interest.

Micrographics Newsletter. Larchmont, N.Y.: Microfilm Publishing, Inc., all issues will be of interest.

O'Toole, James M. *Understanding Archives and Manuscripts.* Chicago: Society of American Archivists, 1990.

Palmer, Roger C. *The Bar Code Book.* Peterborough, N.H.: Helmers Publishing, Inc., 1994.

Peck, Janice L., and Florence M. Ochsner. *Records Retention Guidelines for U.S. Based Real Estate Organizations.* Prairie Village, Kan.: ARMA International, 1993.

Photography (Chemicals)—Residual Thisosulfate and Other Chemicals in Films, Plates and Papers—Determination and Measurement, ANSI PH4.8-1985. Silver Spring, Md.: AIIM, 1985.

Photography (Film)—Processed Safety Film—Storage, ANSI PH1.43-1985. Silver Spring, Md.: AIIM, 1985.

Practice for Operational Procedures/Inspection and Quality Control of First-Generation Silver-Gelatin Microfilm of Documents, ANSI/AIIM MS 23-1983. Silver Spring, Md.: AIIM, 1983.

Protection of Records (NFPA 232). Quincy, Mass.: National Fire Protection Association, latest edition.

Quality Management and Quality Assurance Standards—Guidelines for Selection and Use (ANSI-ASQC Q9000-1-1994). Milwaukee: American Society for Quality Control, 1994.

Quality Management and Quality System Elements—Guidelines (ANSI/ASQC Q9004-1-1994). Milwaukee: American Society for Quality Control, 1994.

Quality Systems—Model for Quality Assurance in Design, Development, Production, Installation, and Servicing (ANSI-ASQC Q9001-1994). Milwaukee: American Society for Quality Control, 1994.

Quality Systems—Model for Quality Assurance in Final Inspection and Test (ANSI-ASQC Q9003-1994). Milwaukee: American Society for Quality Control, 1994.

Quality Systems—Model for Quality Assurance in Production, Installation, and Servicing (ANSI-ASQC Q9002-1994). Milwaukee: American Society for Quality Control, 1994.

Recommended Practice for Inspection of Stored Microfilm, ANSI/AIIM MS 45-1990. Silver Spring, Md.: AIIM, 1990.

Records Management Quarterly. Prairie Village, Kan.: ARMA International, all issues will be of interest.

Saffady, William. *Managing Electronic Records.* Prairie Village, Kan.: ARMA International, 1992.

Saffady, William. *Micrographic Systems.* Silver Spring, Md.: AIIM, 1990.

Skupsky, Donald S., ed. *Legal Requirements for Business Records.* Denver: Information Records Clearinghouse, updated annually.

Skupsky, Donald S., *Legal Requirements for Microfilm, Computer and Optical Disk Records.* Denver: Information Records Clearinghouse, latest edition.

Skupsky, Donald S. *Recordkeeping Requirements.* Denver: Information Records Clearinghouse, latest edition.

Software Directory for Automated Records Management Systems. Prairie Village, Kan.: ARMA International, latest edition.

Weiss, Joseph W., and Robert K. Wysocki. *5-Phase Project Management: A Practical Planning and Implementation Guide.* Reading, Mass.: Addison-Wesley Publishing Company, Inc., 1992.

Index